About this book:

This is a collection of my Inktober 2018 drawings.
If you're not familiar, Inktober is a drawing challenge
created by Mr. Jake Parker. The challenge is to create
an ink drawing for each day of October. This is my
second year participating, and it's still tough to get
through the month.

This year I decided to go for a sea life theme. Not
only because I love fish (as animals not as food) and
other life found underwater, but also as research for
an upcoming project. While it was a lot of fun this
year, it was as challenging as ever. I hope you enjoy
the color versions of the illustrations!

Thanks for your support.

-Nathan Lumm

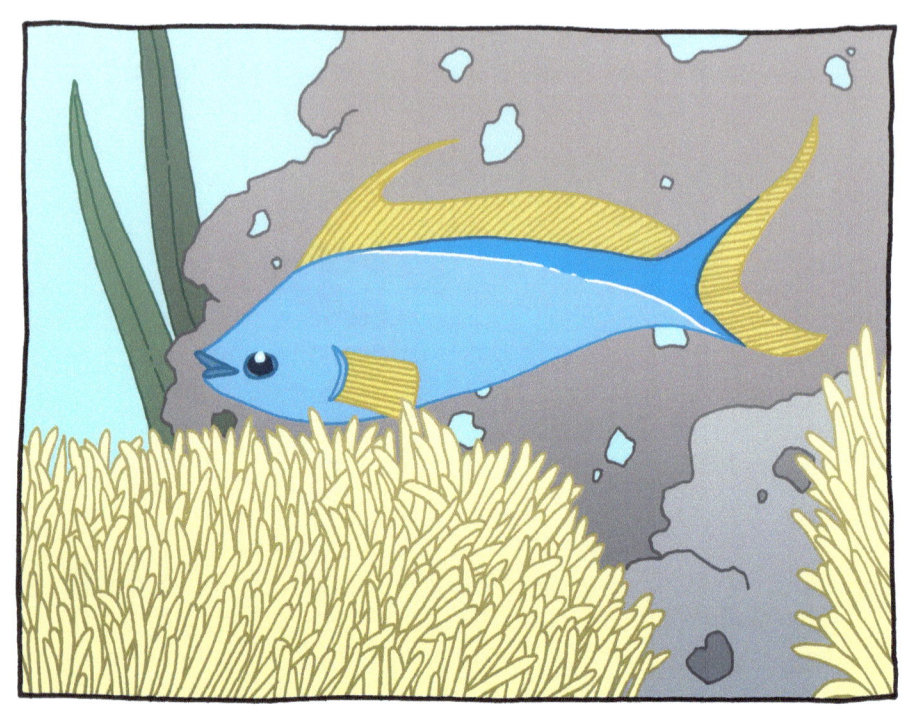

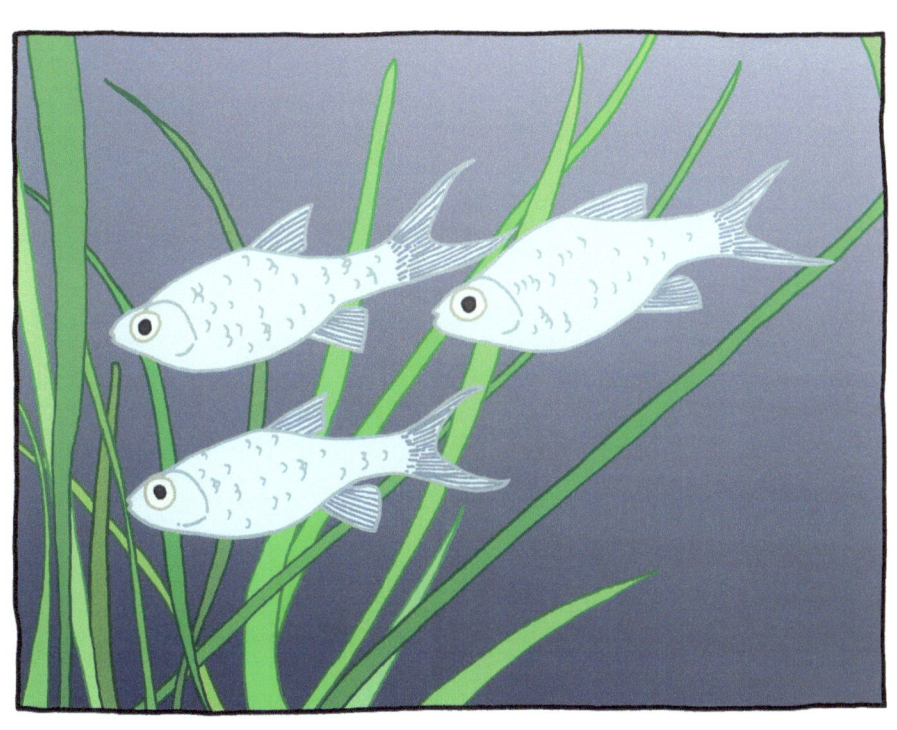

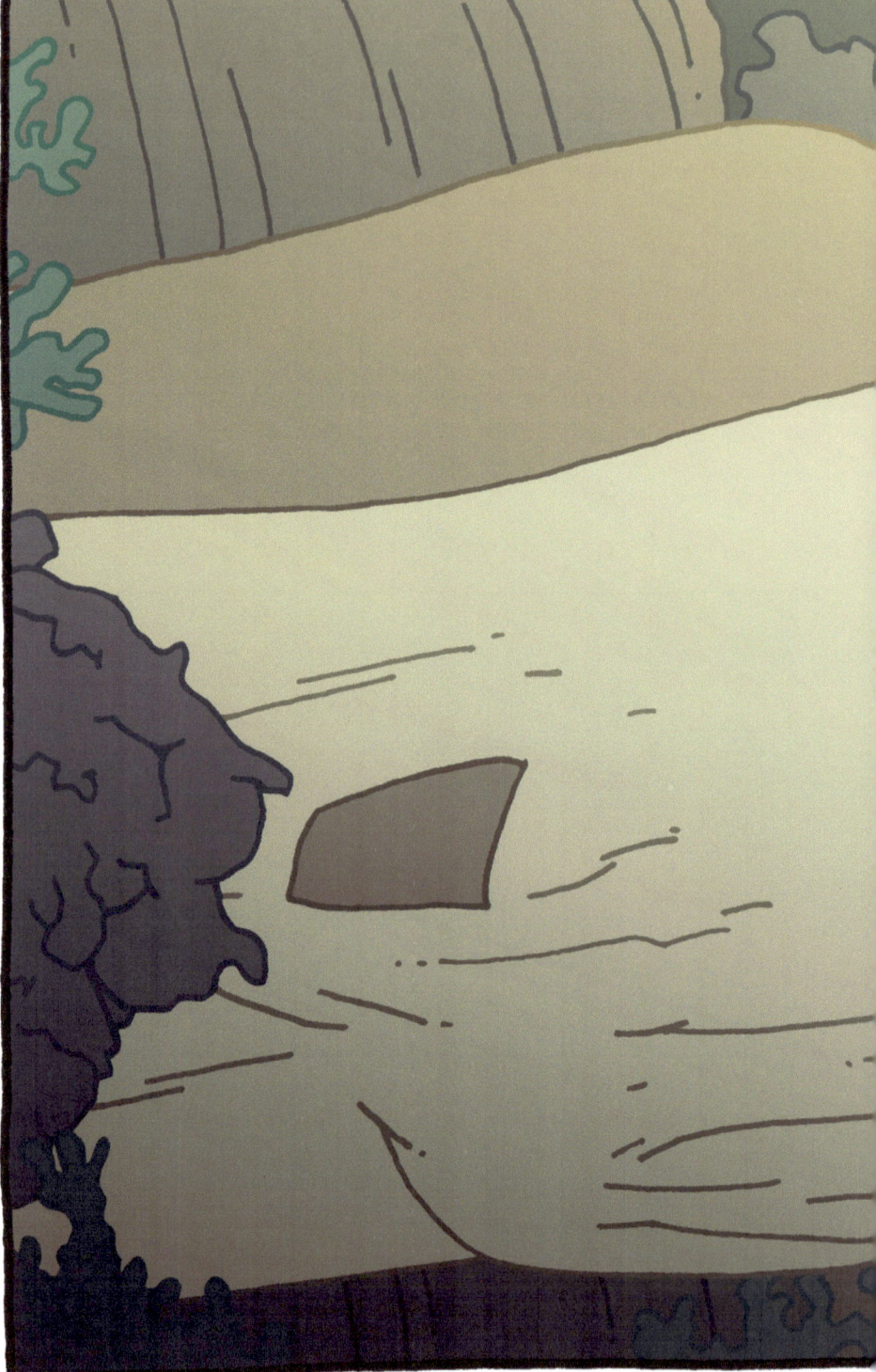

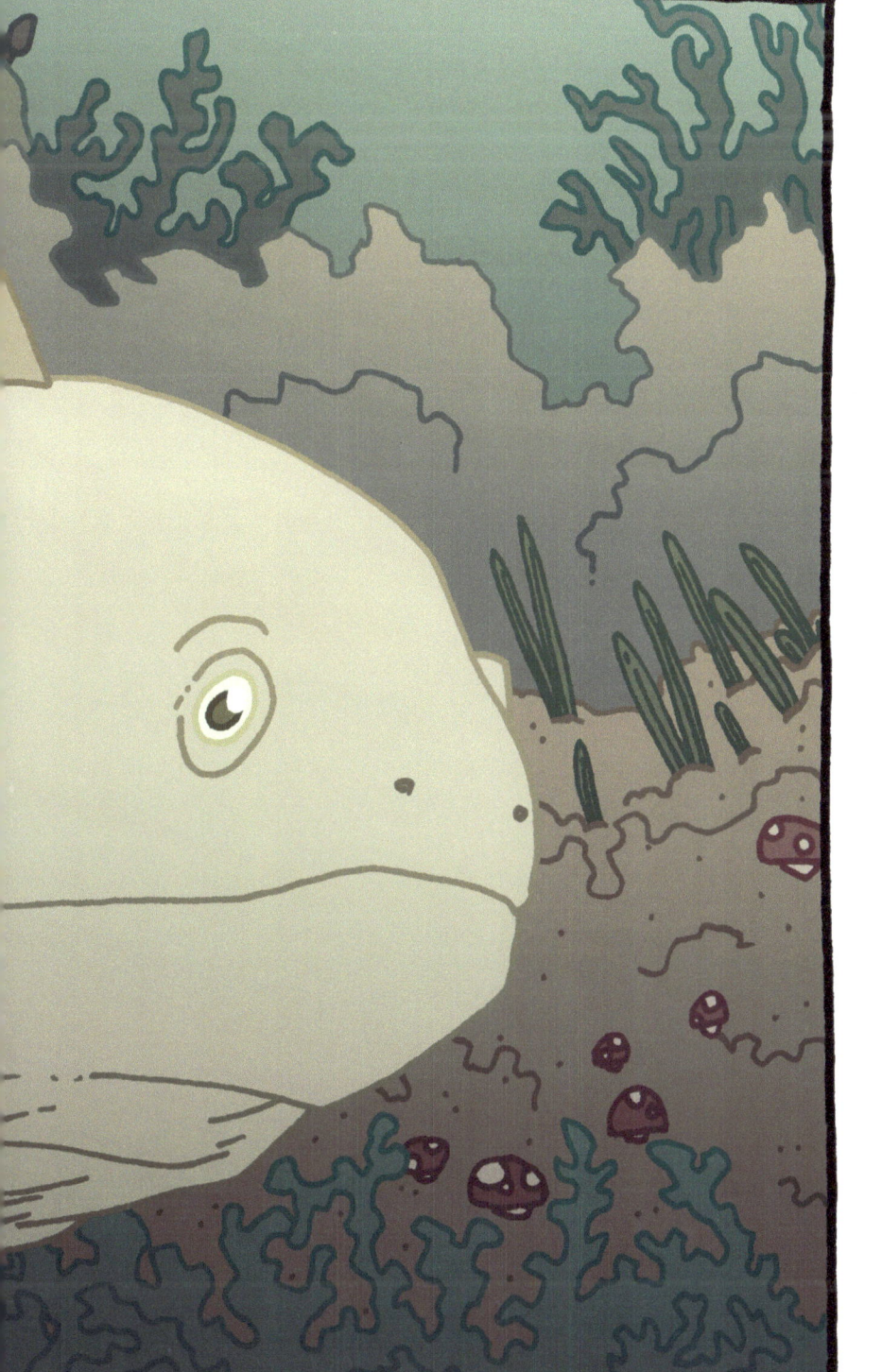

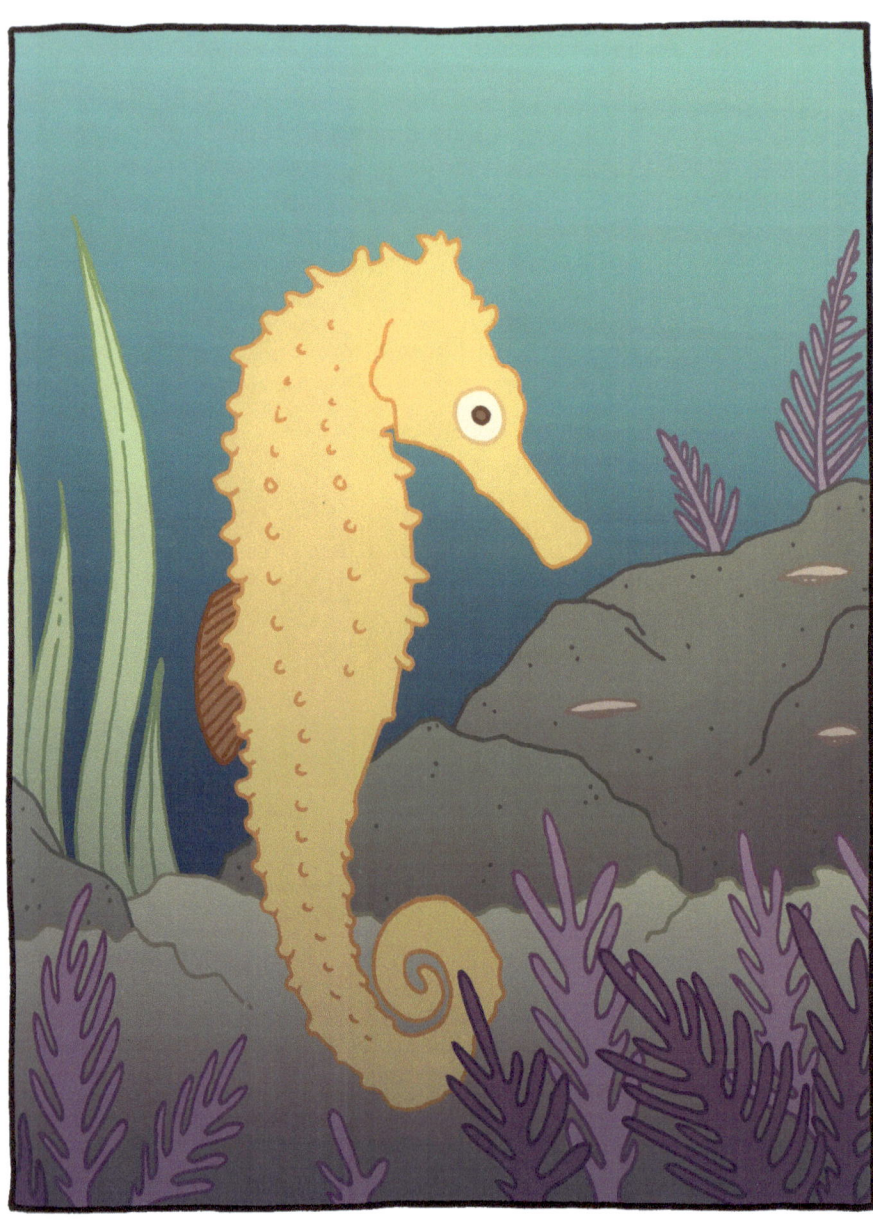

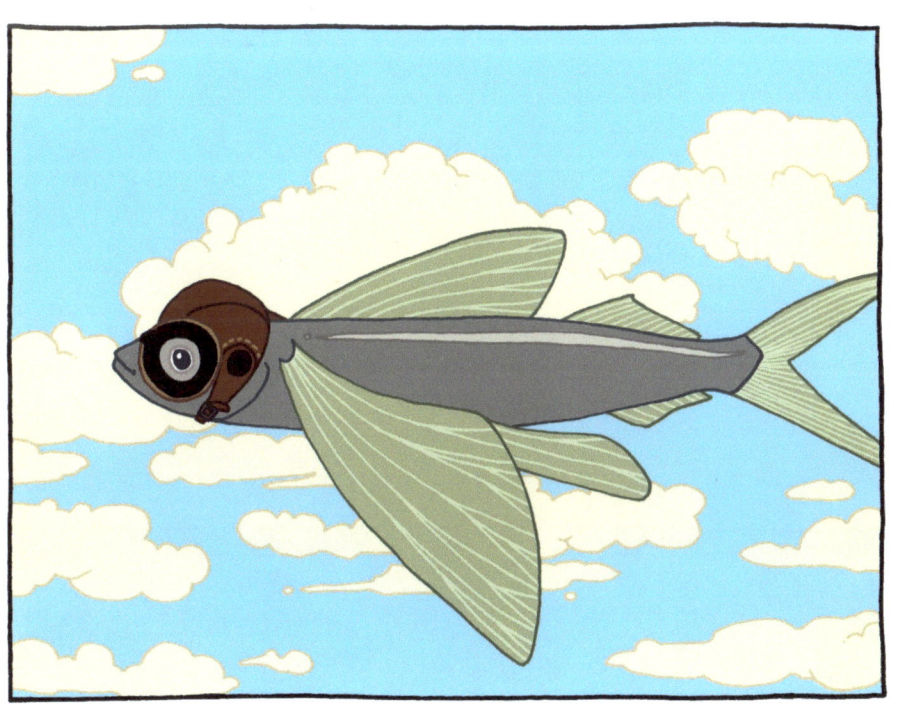

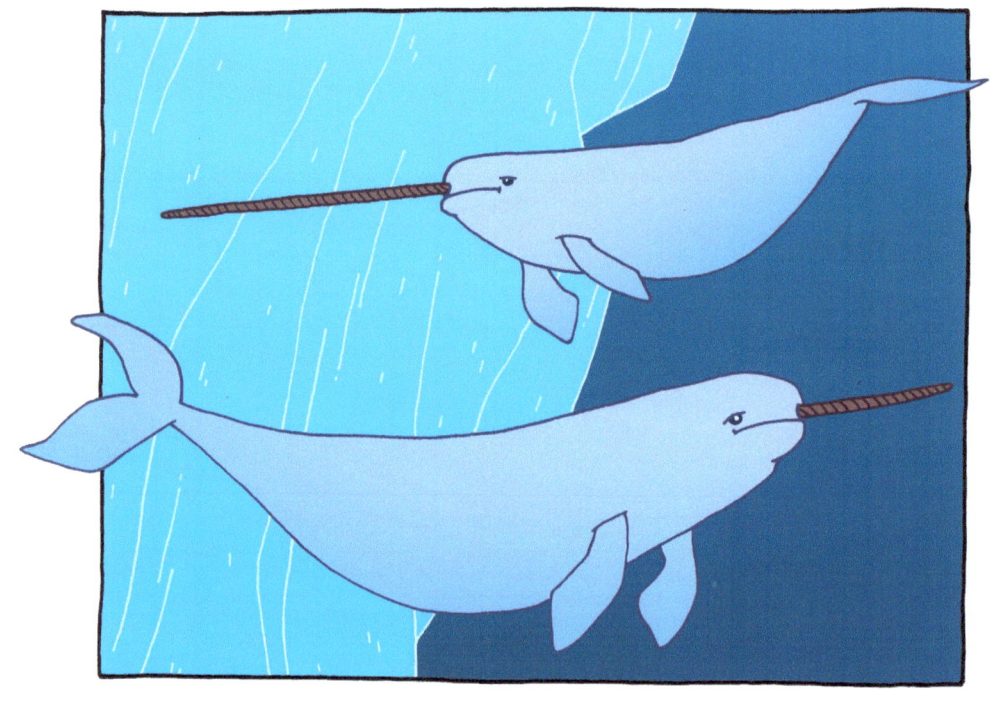

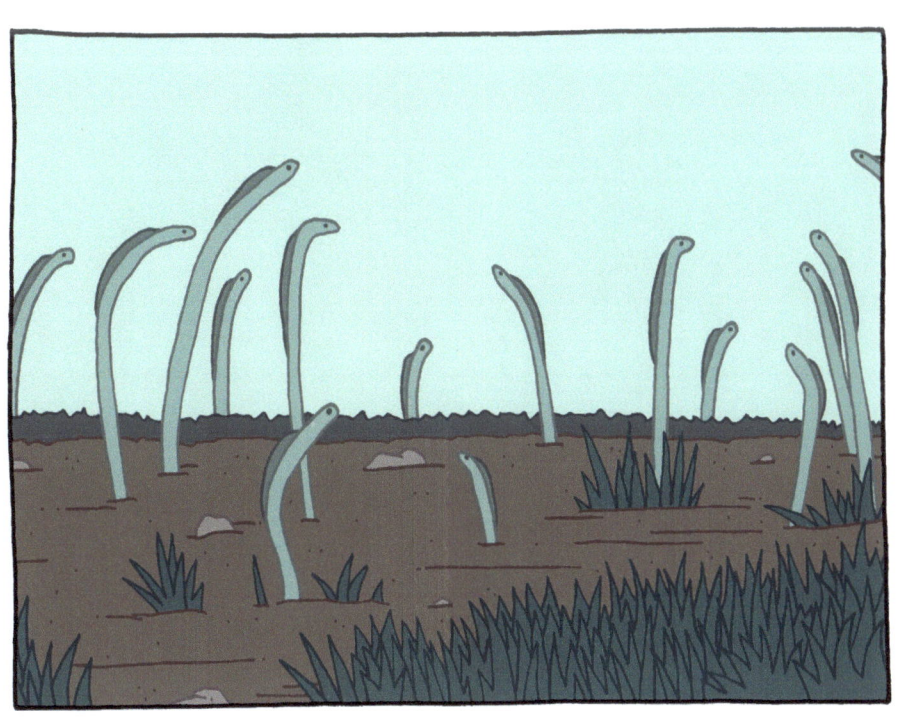

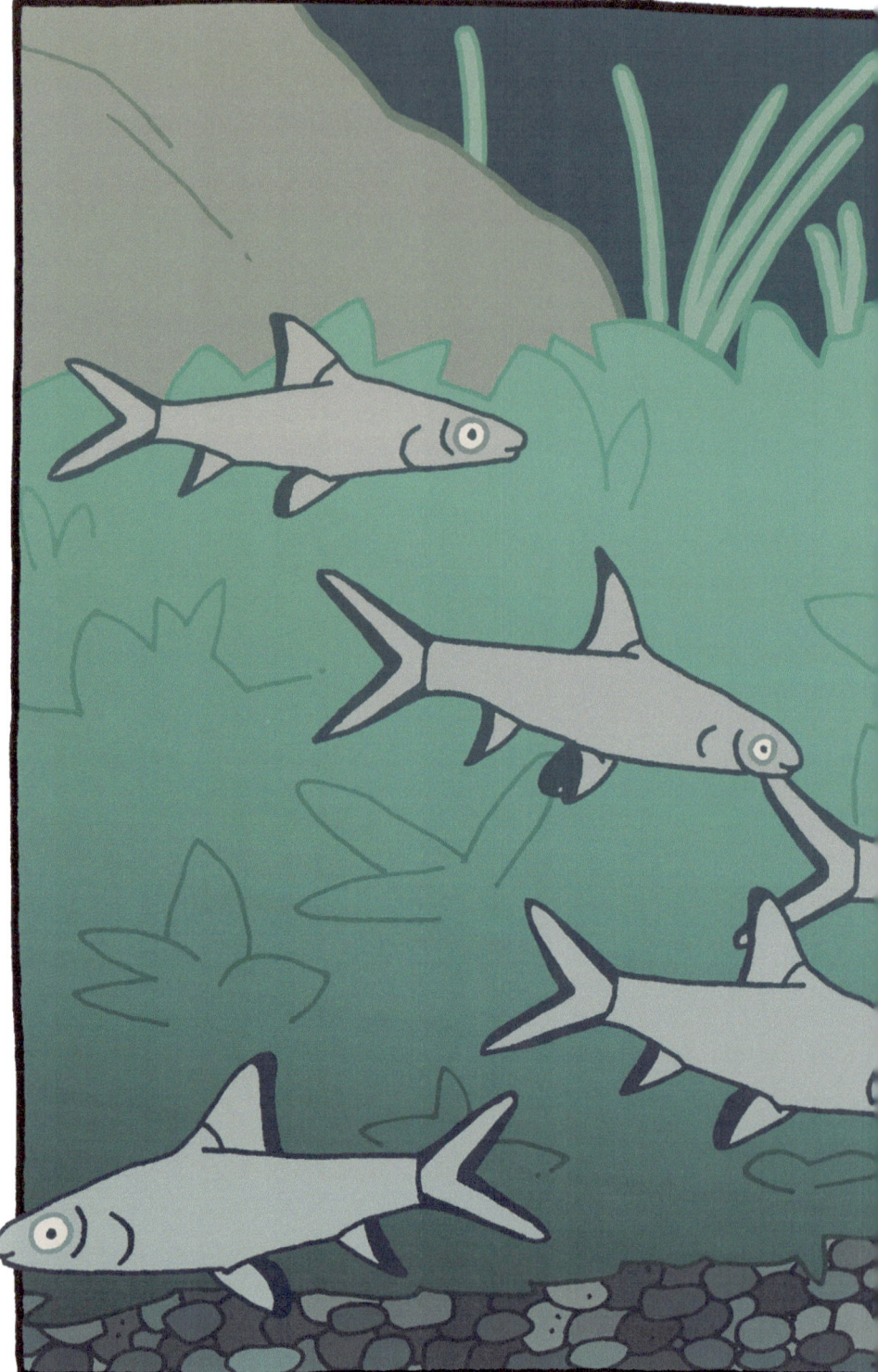

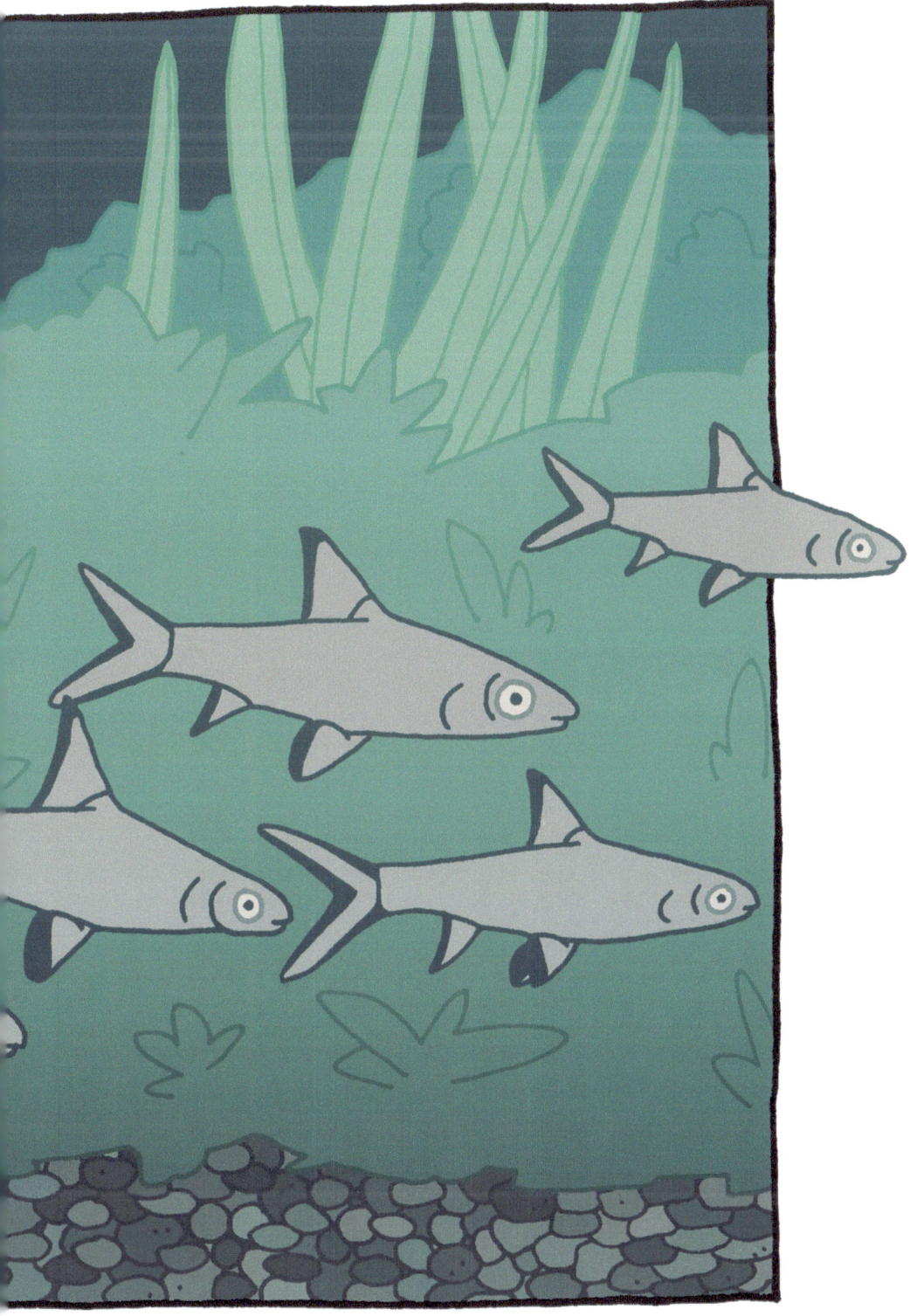

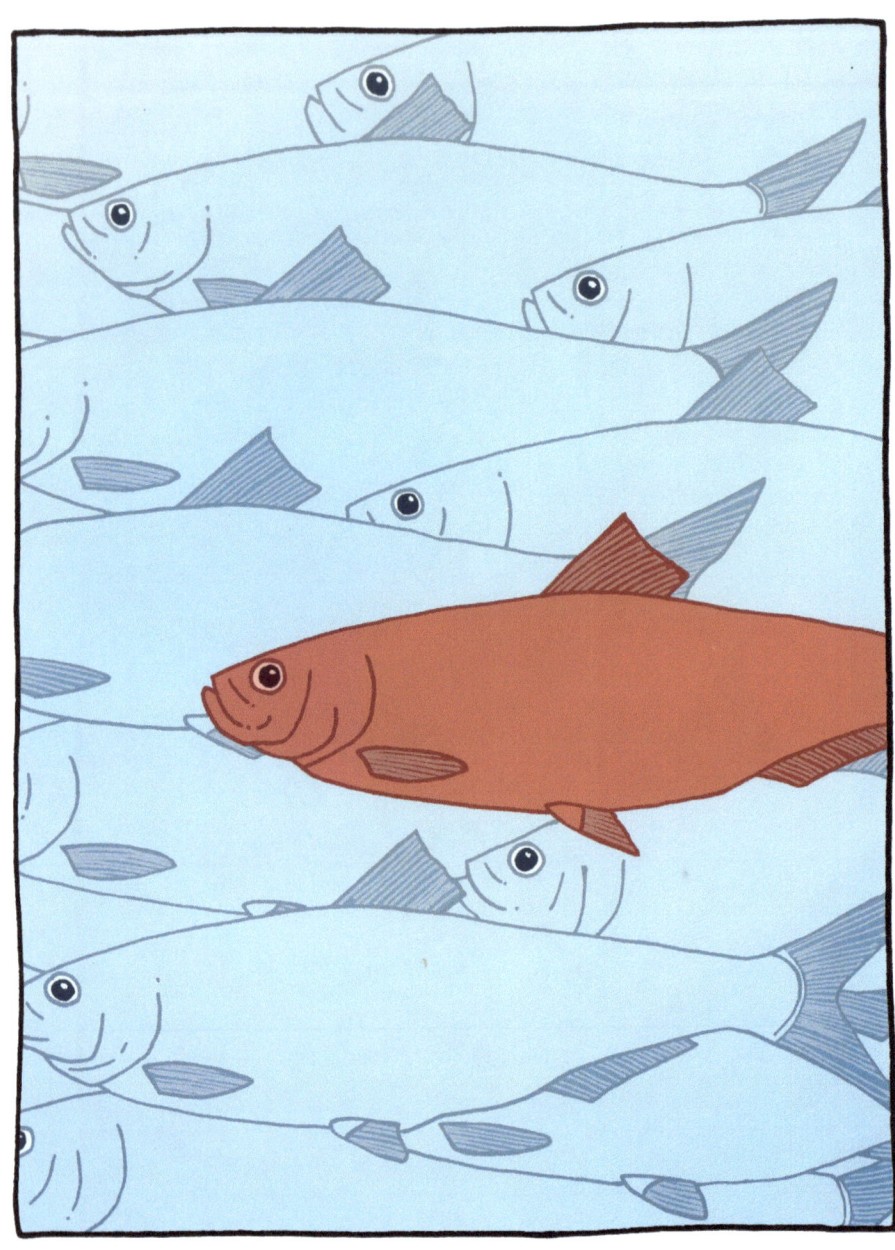

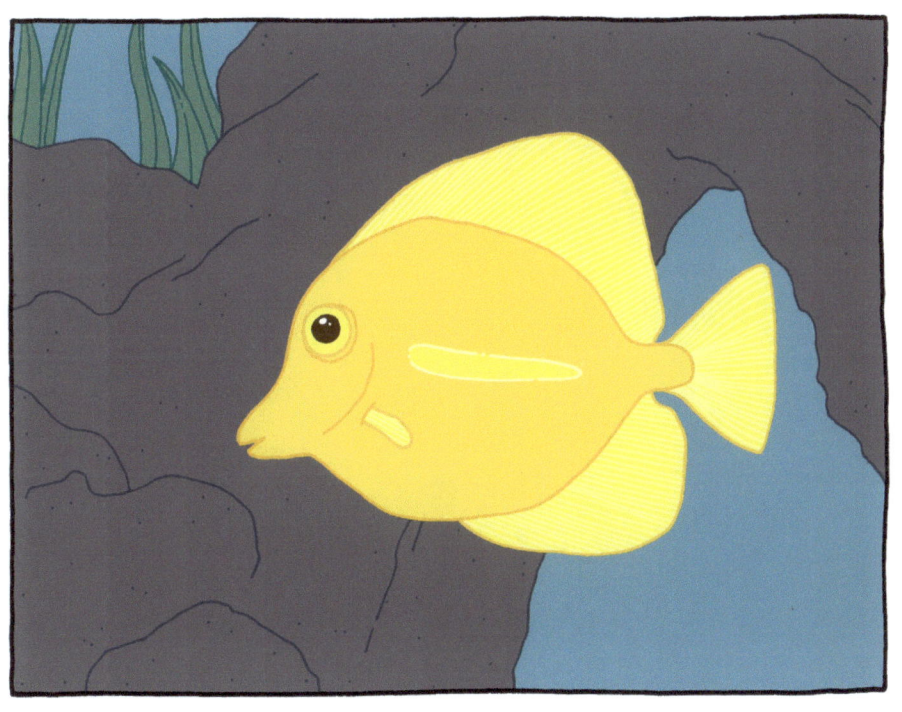

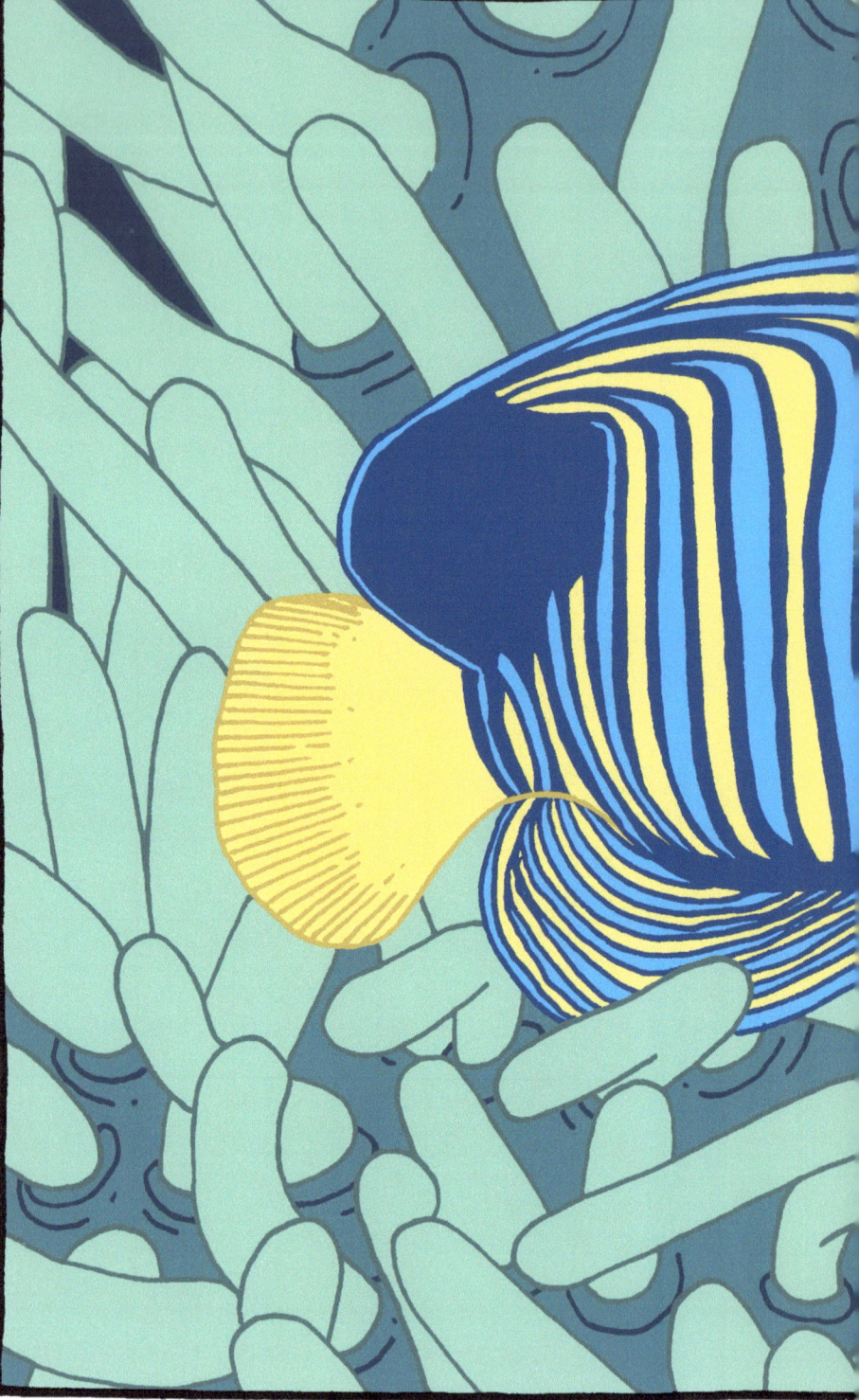

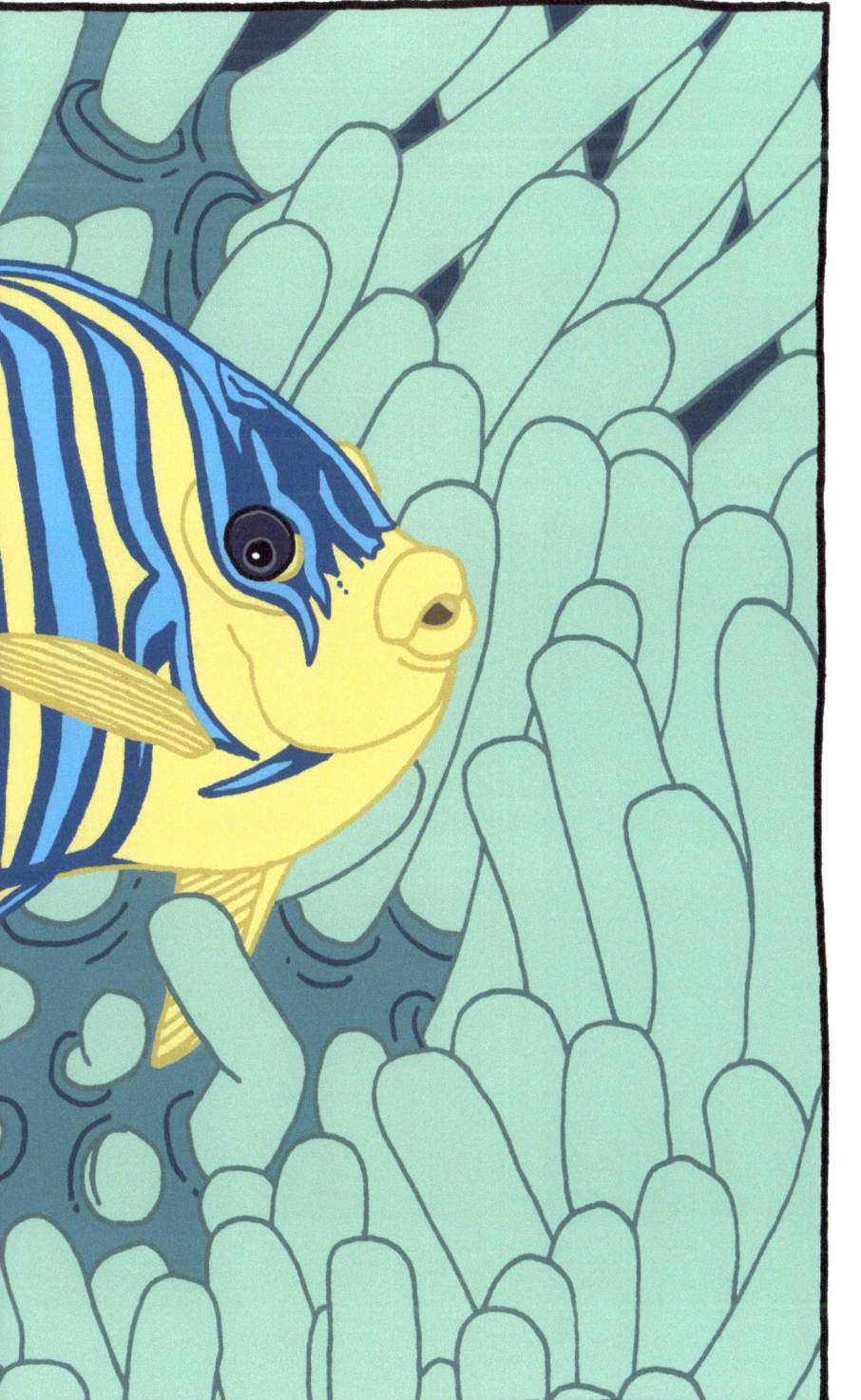

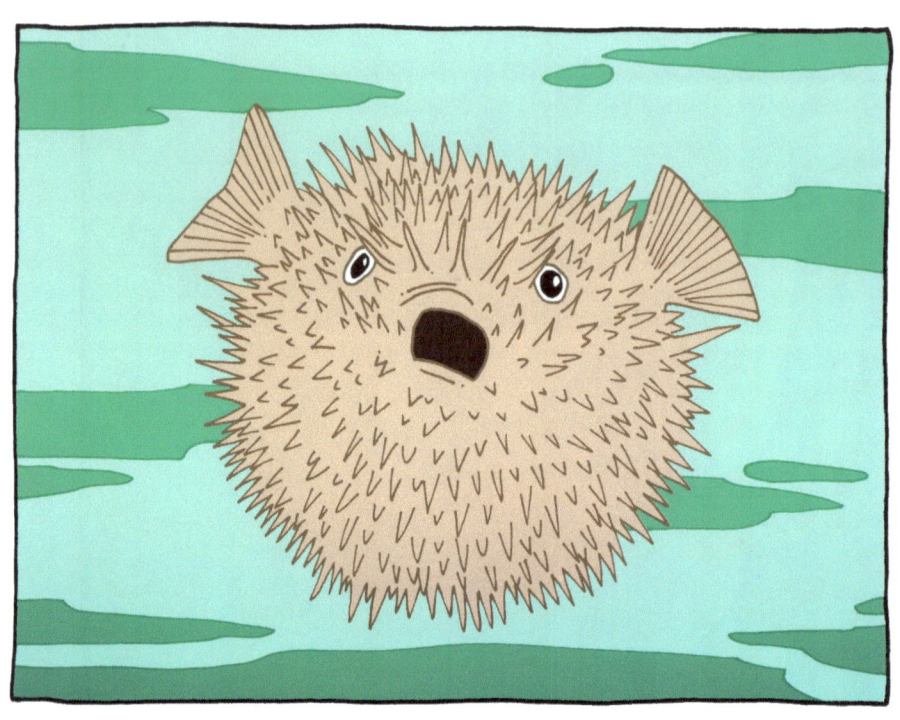

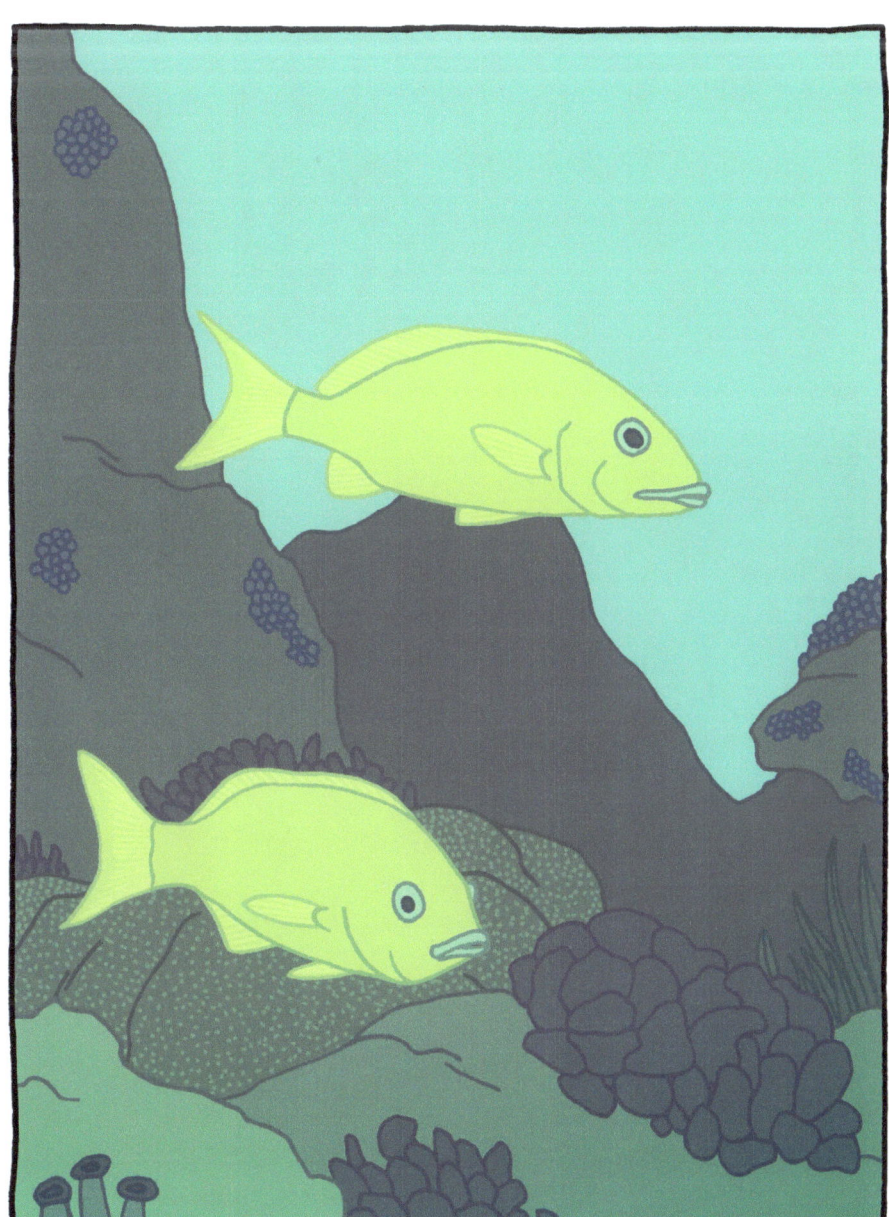

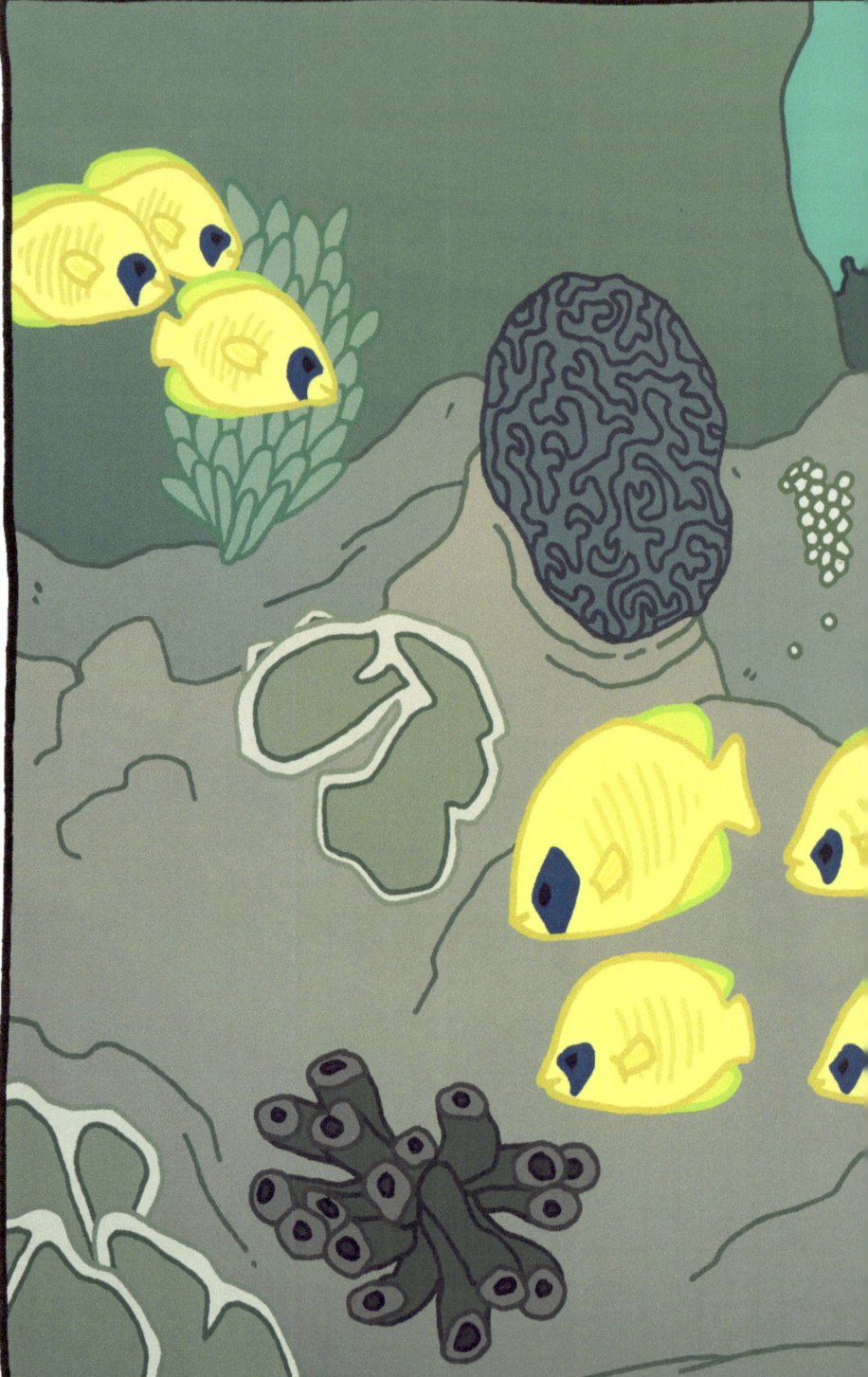

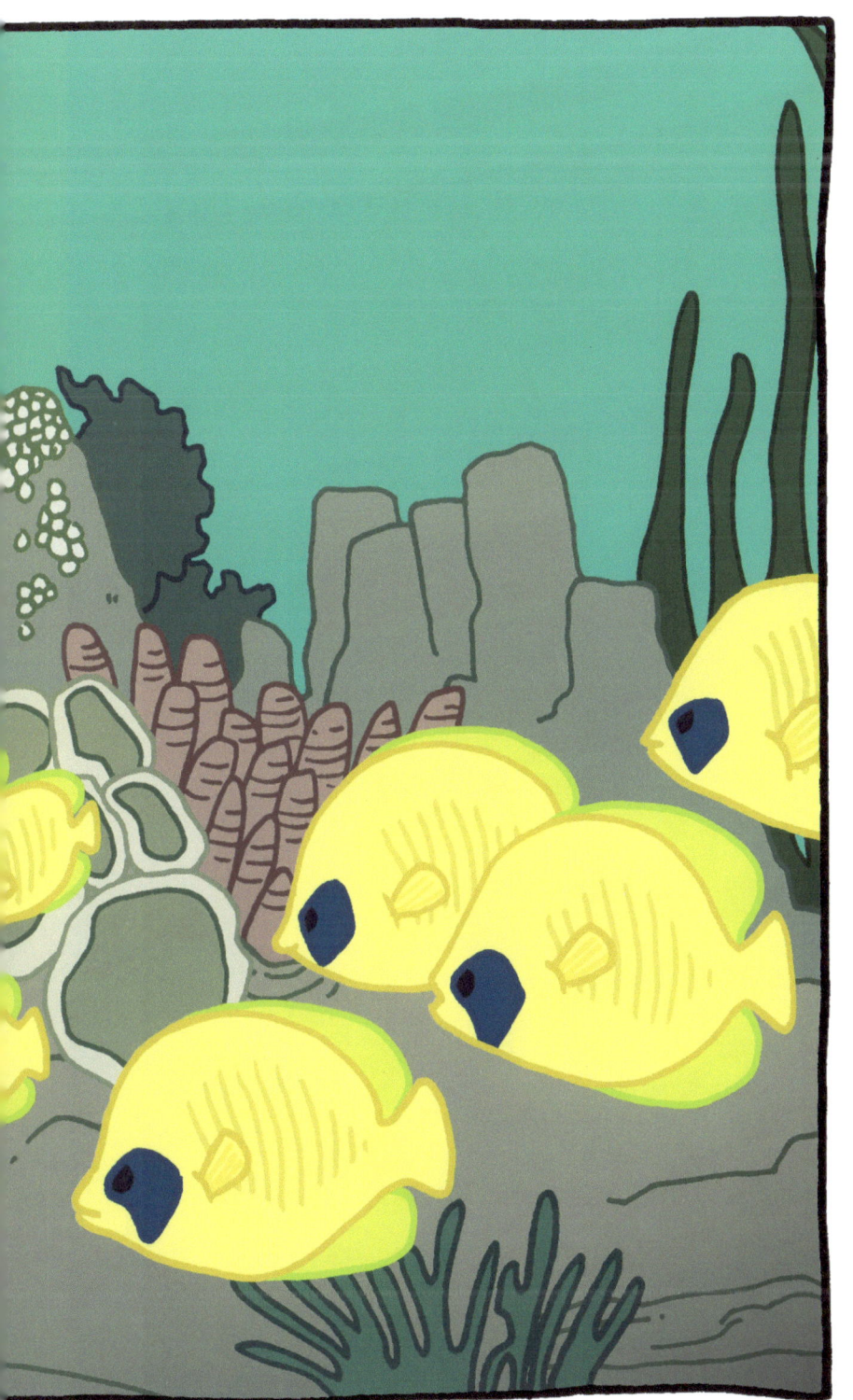

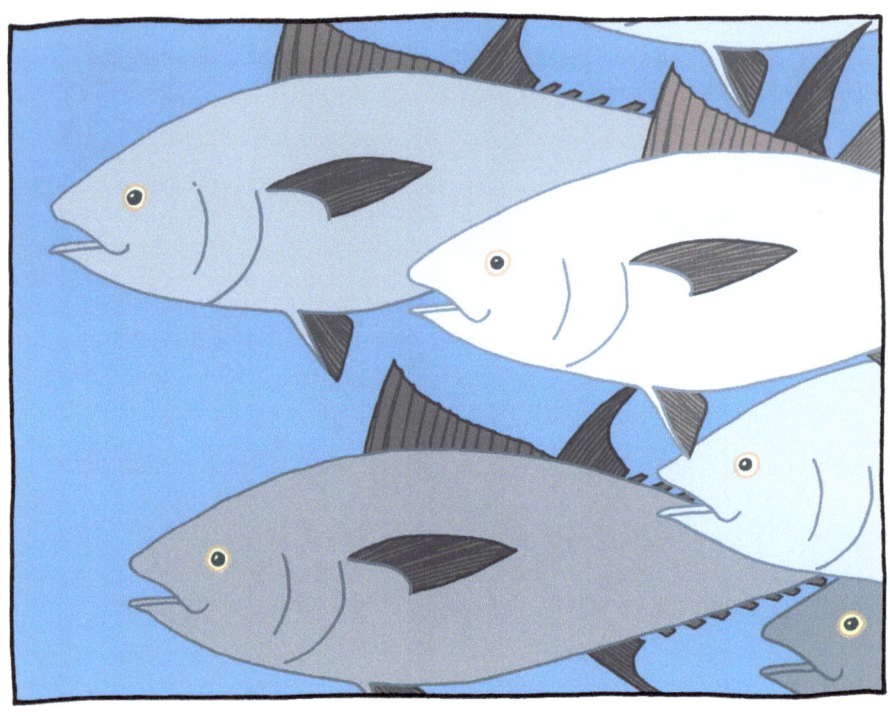

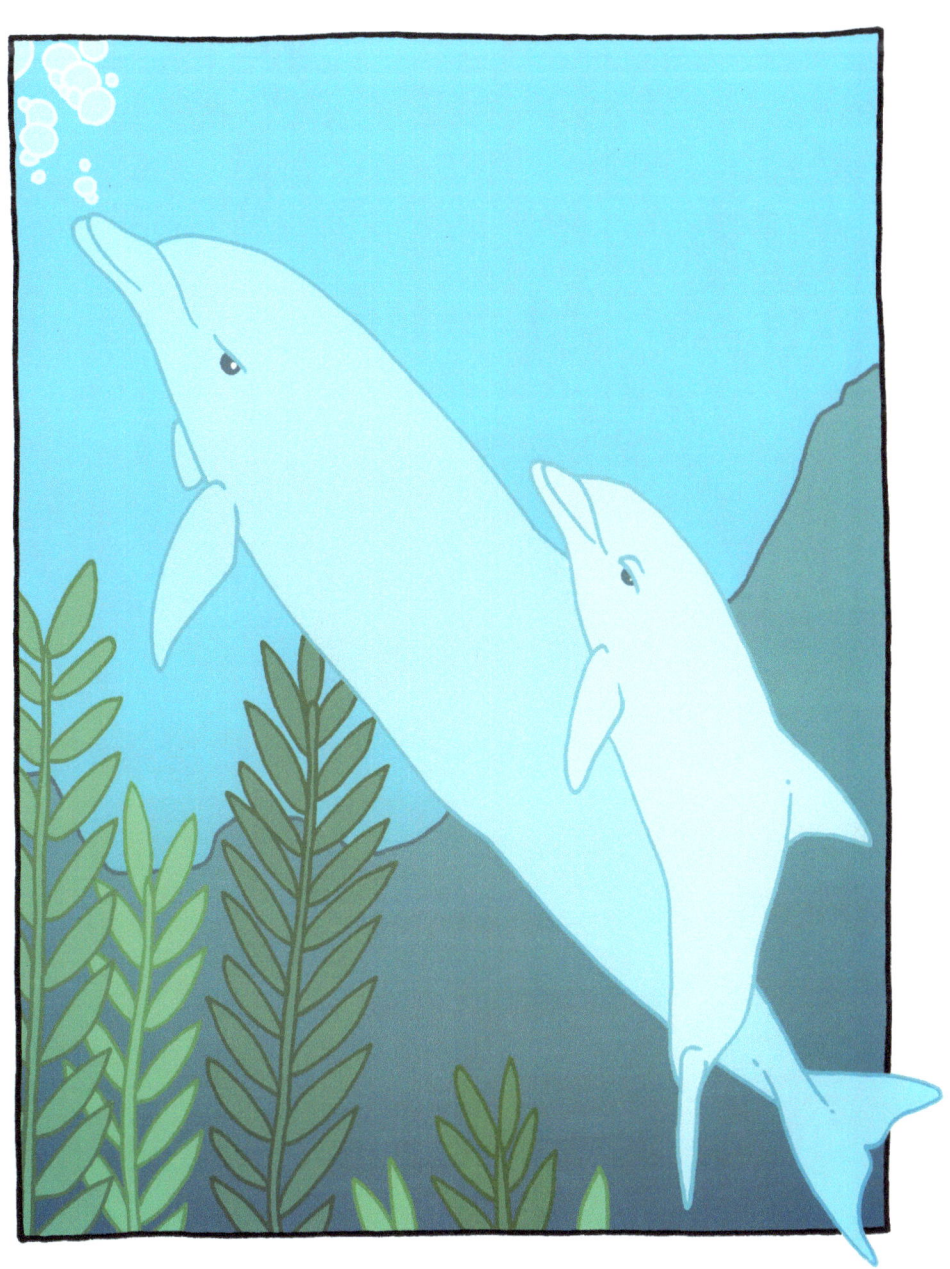

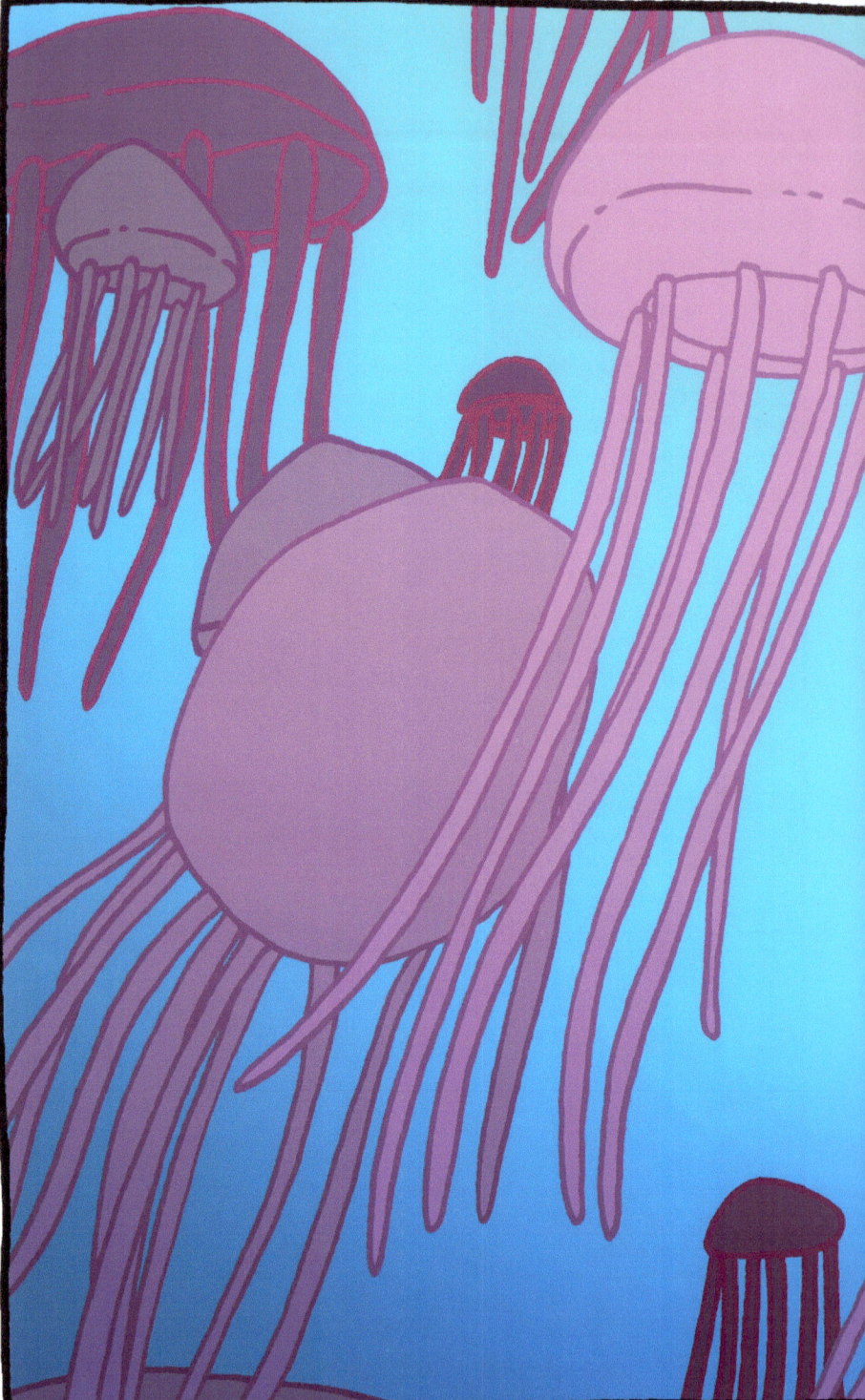

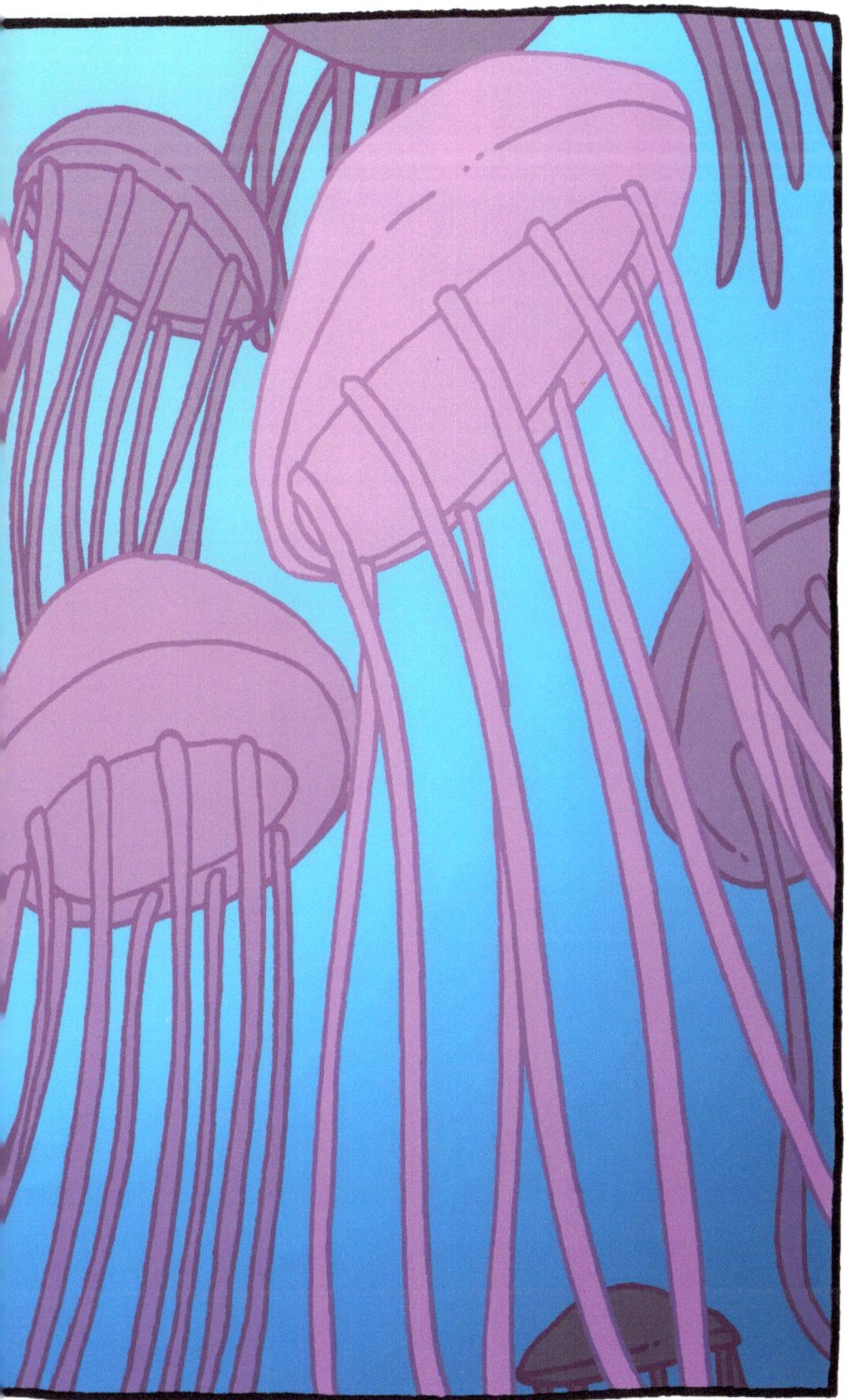

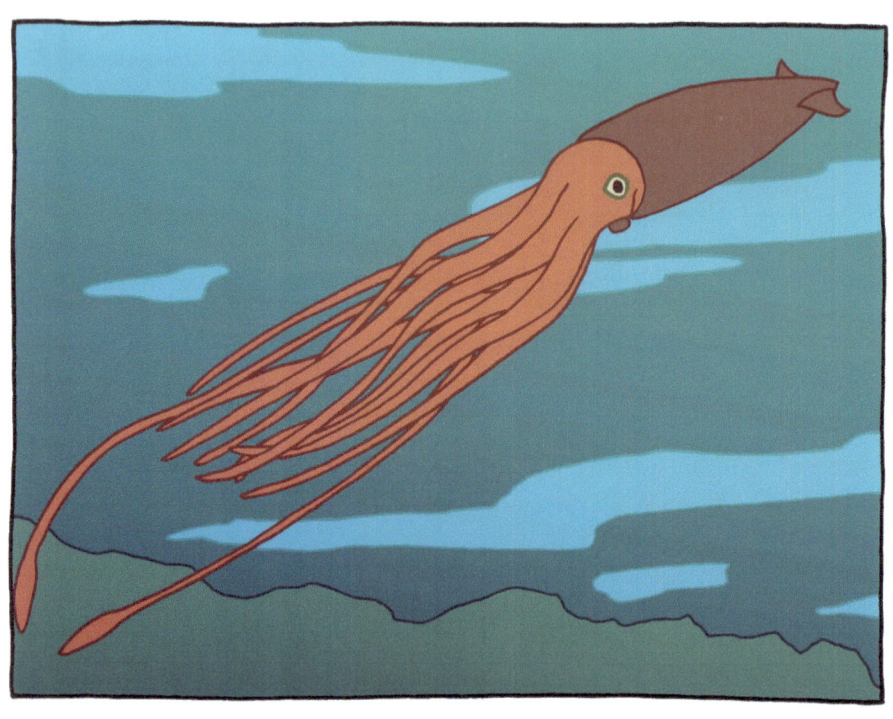

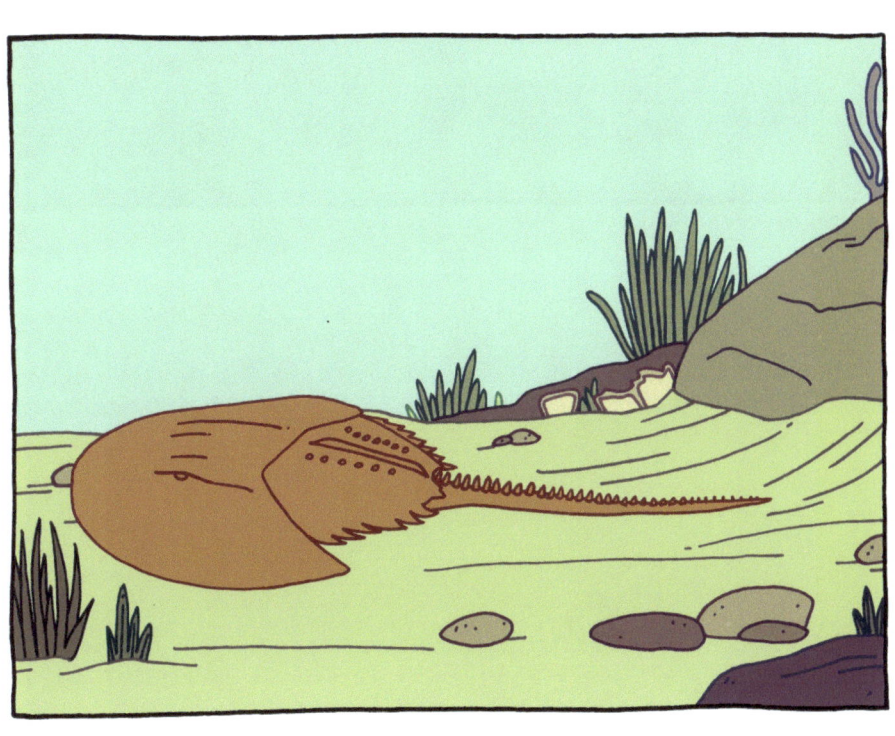

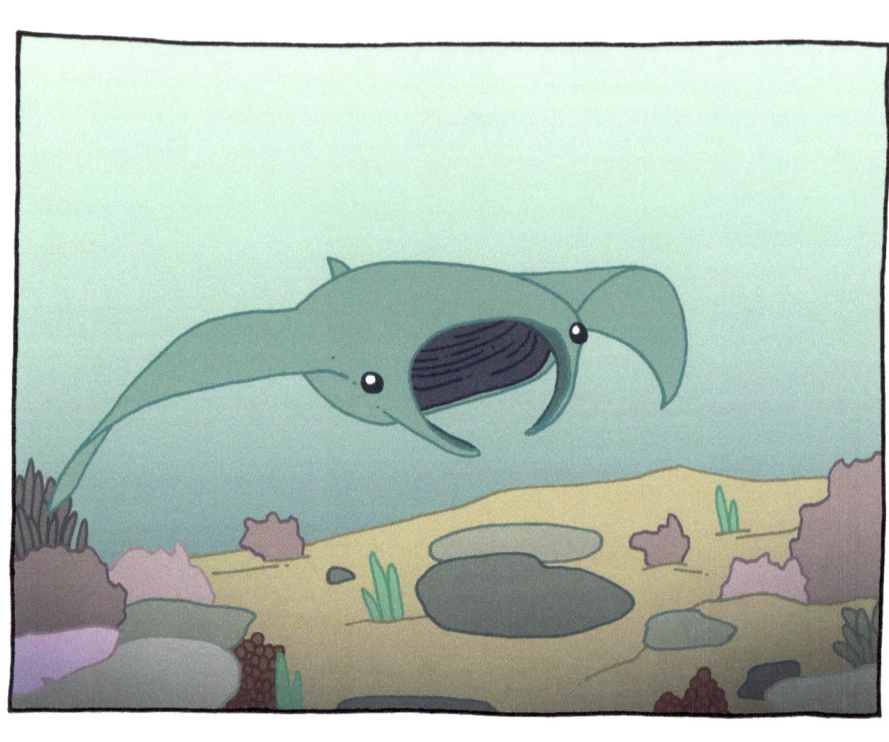

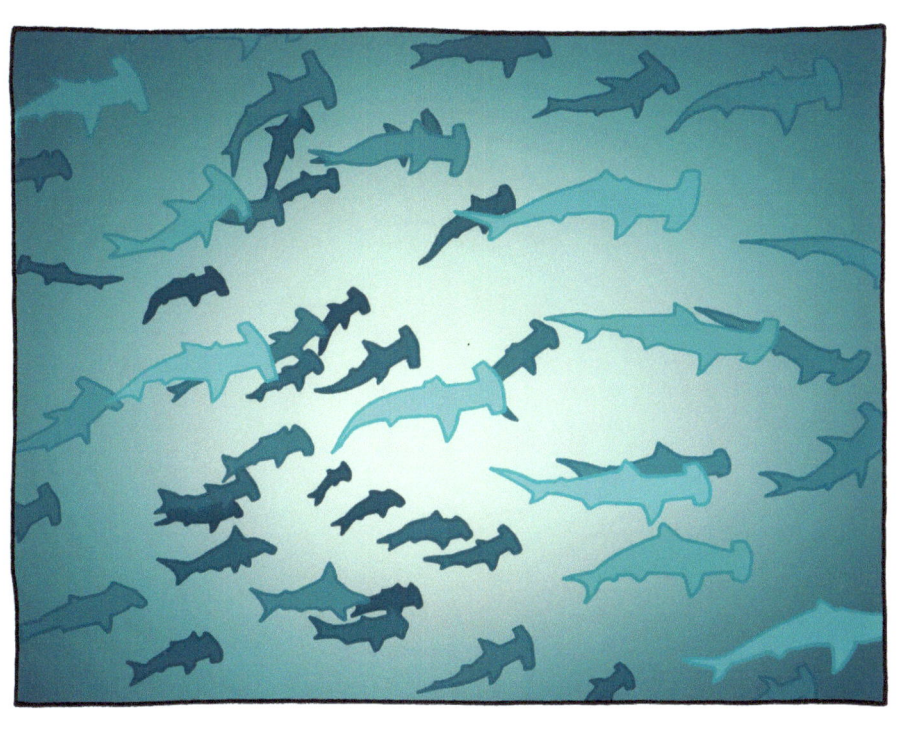

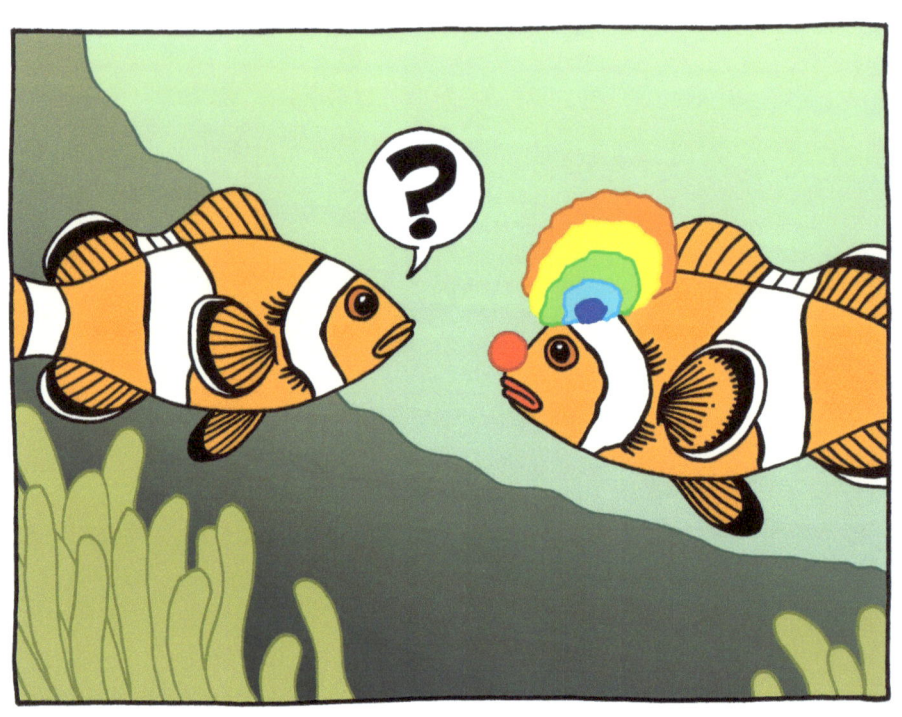

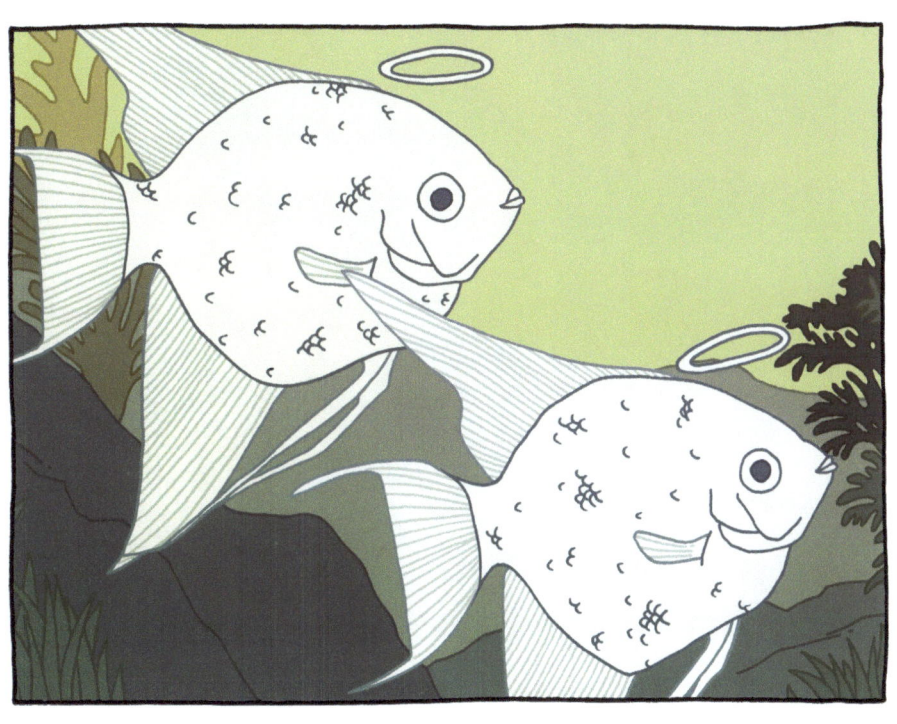

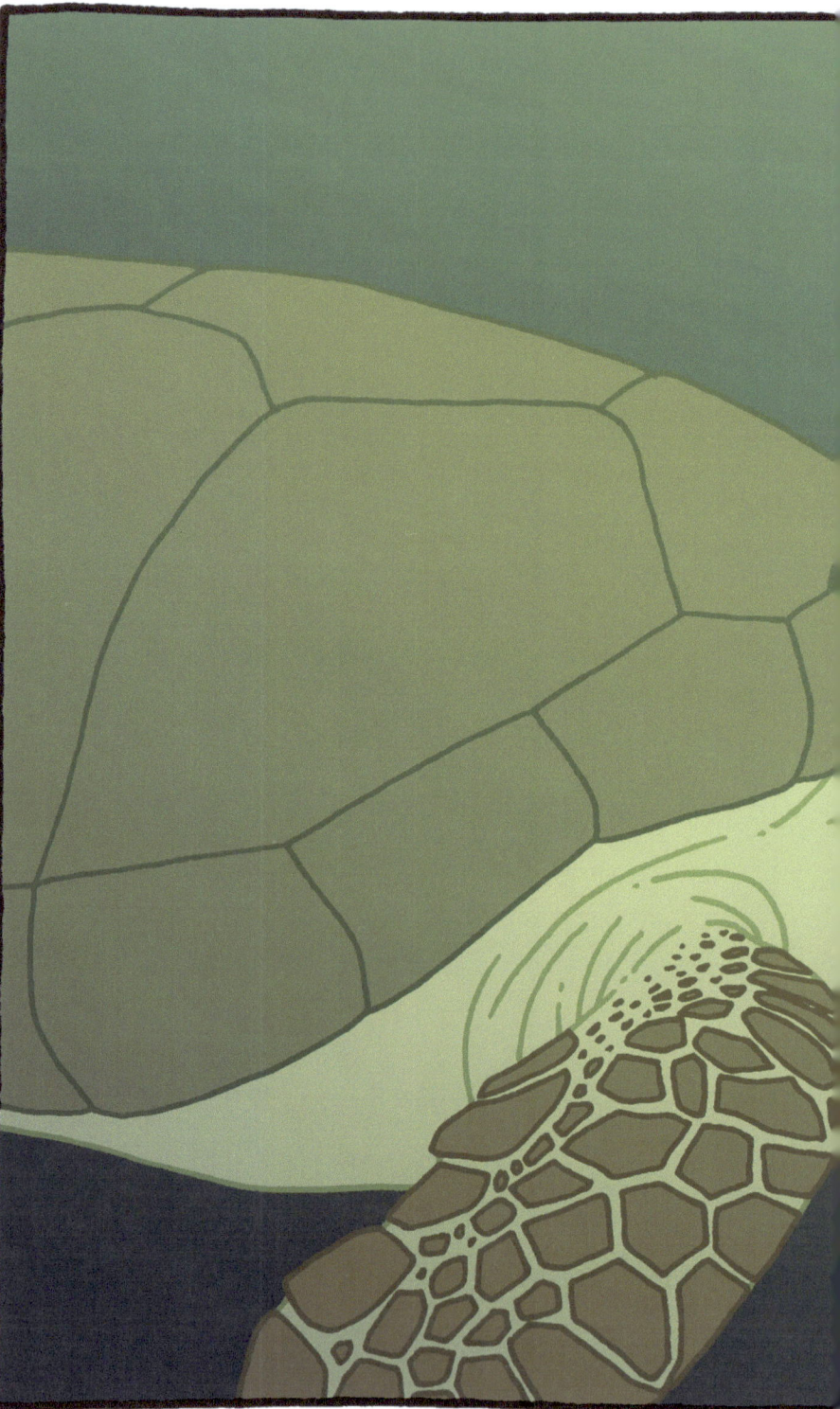

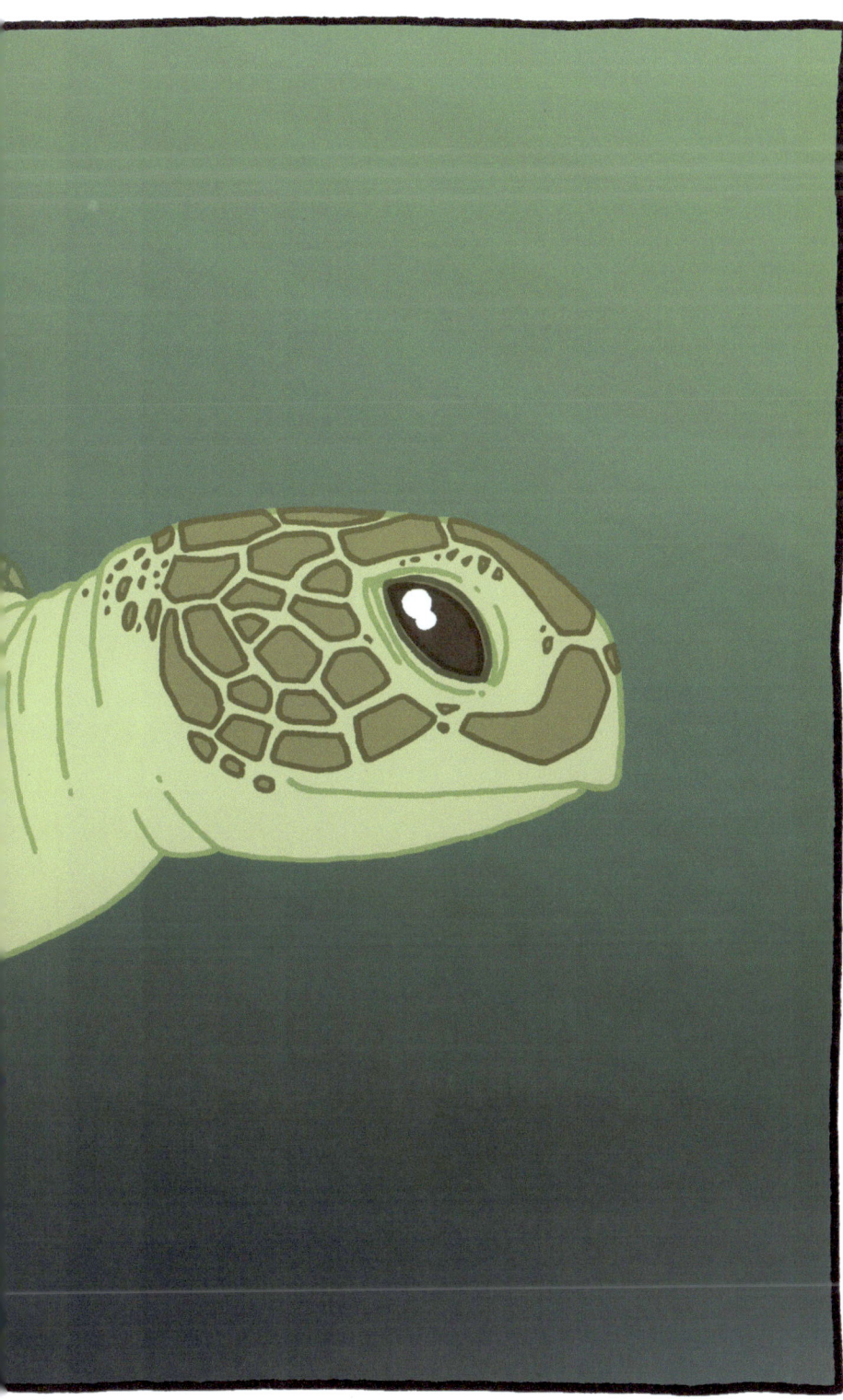

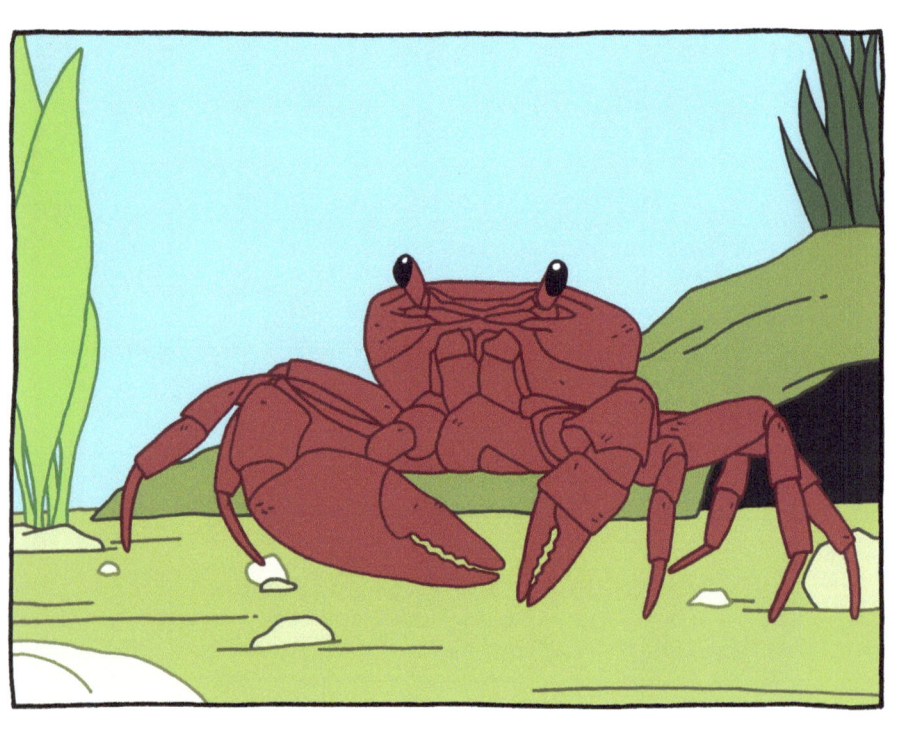

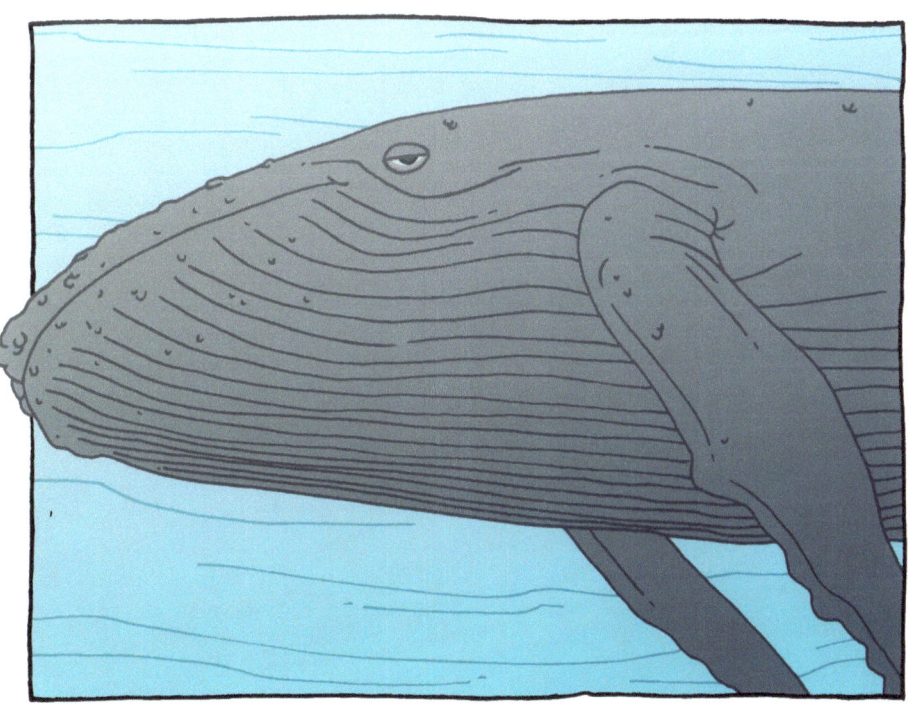

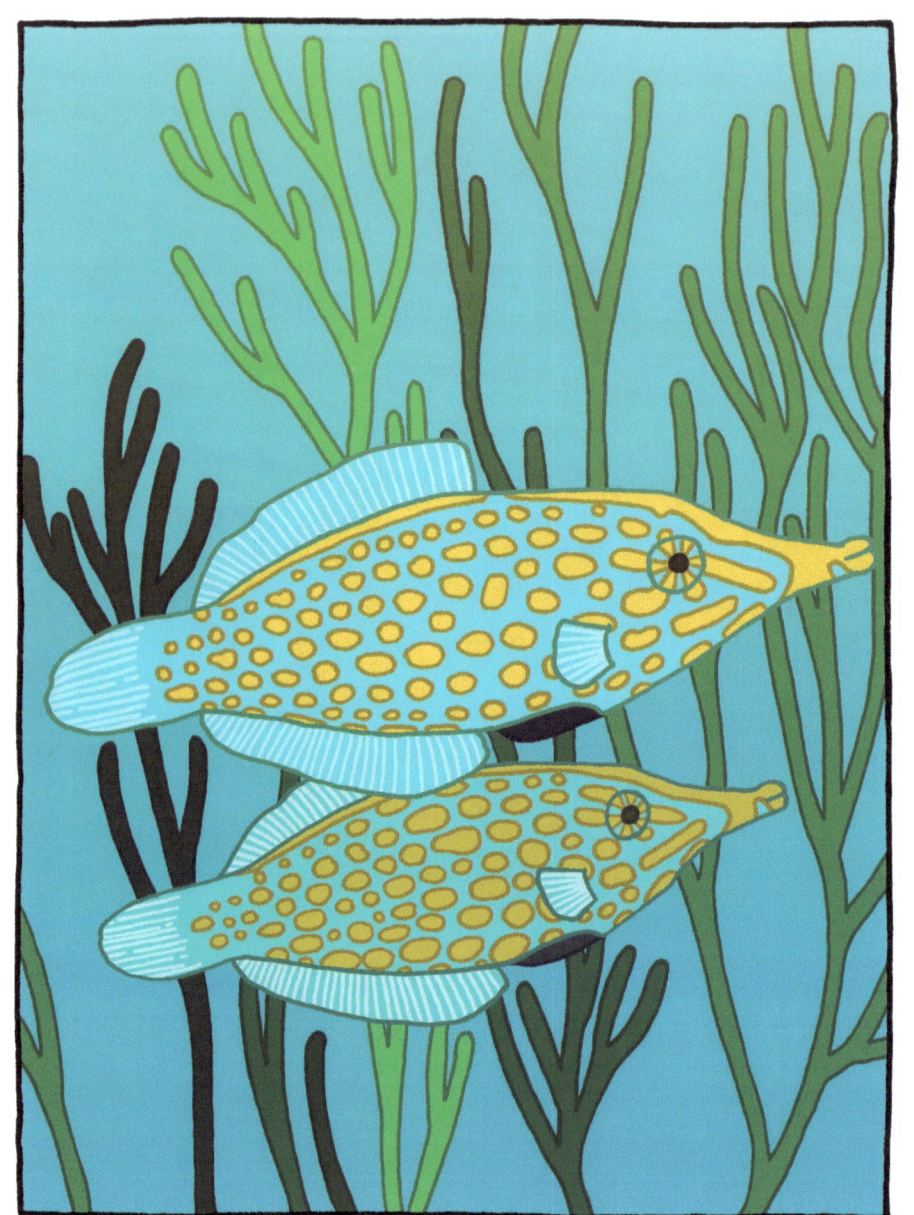

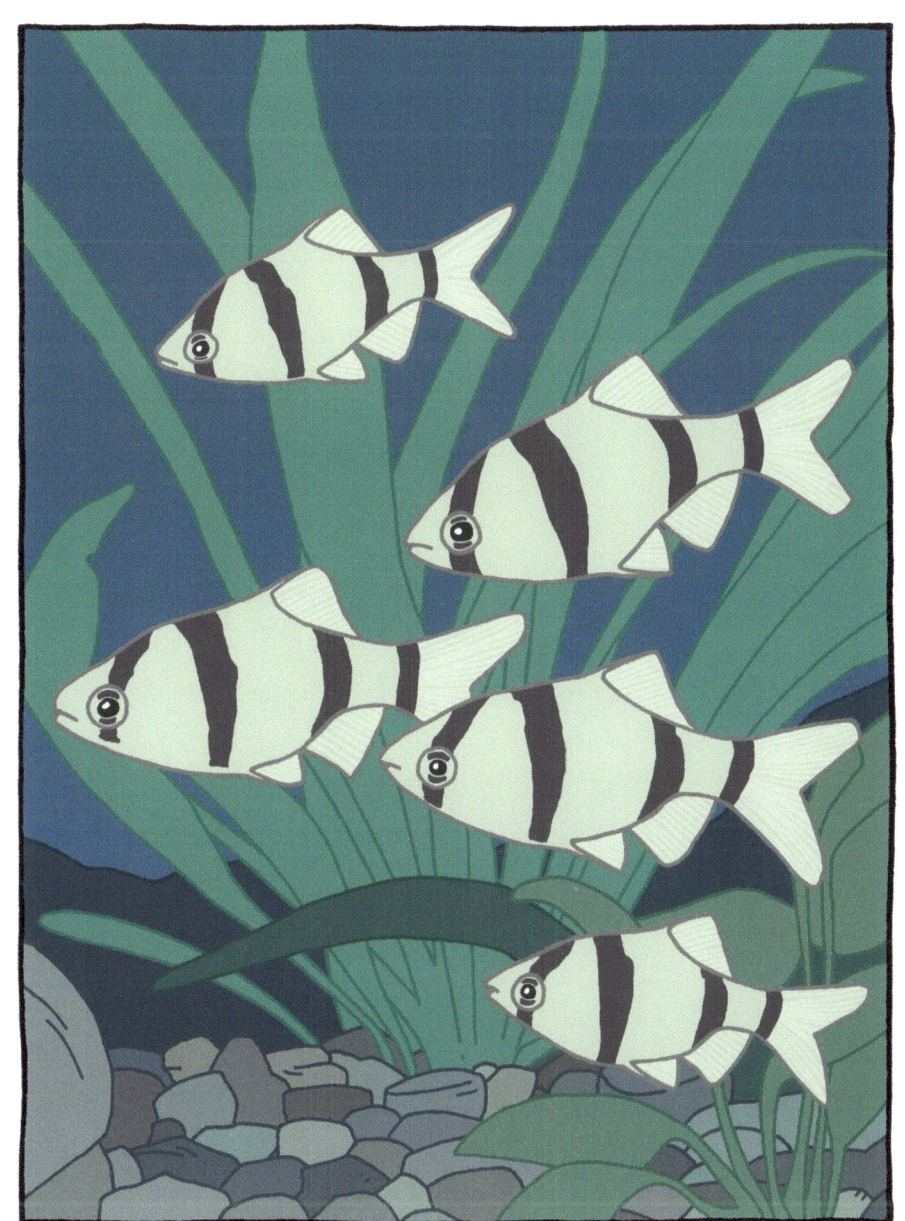

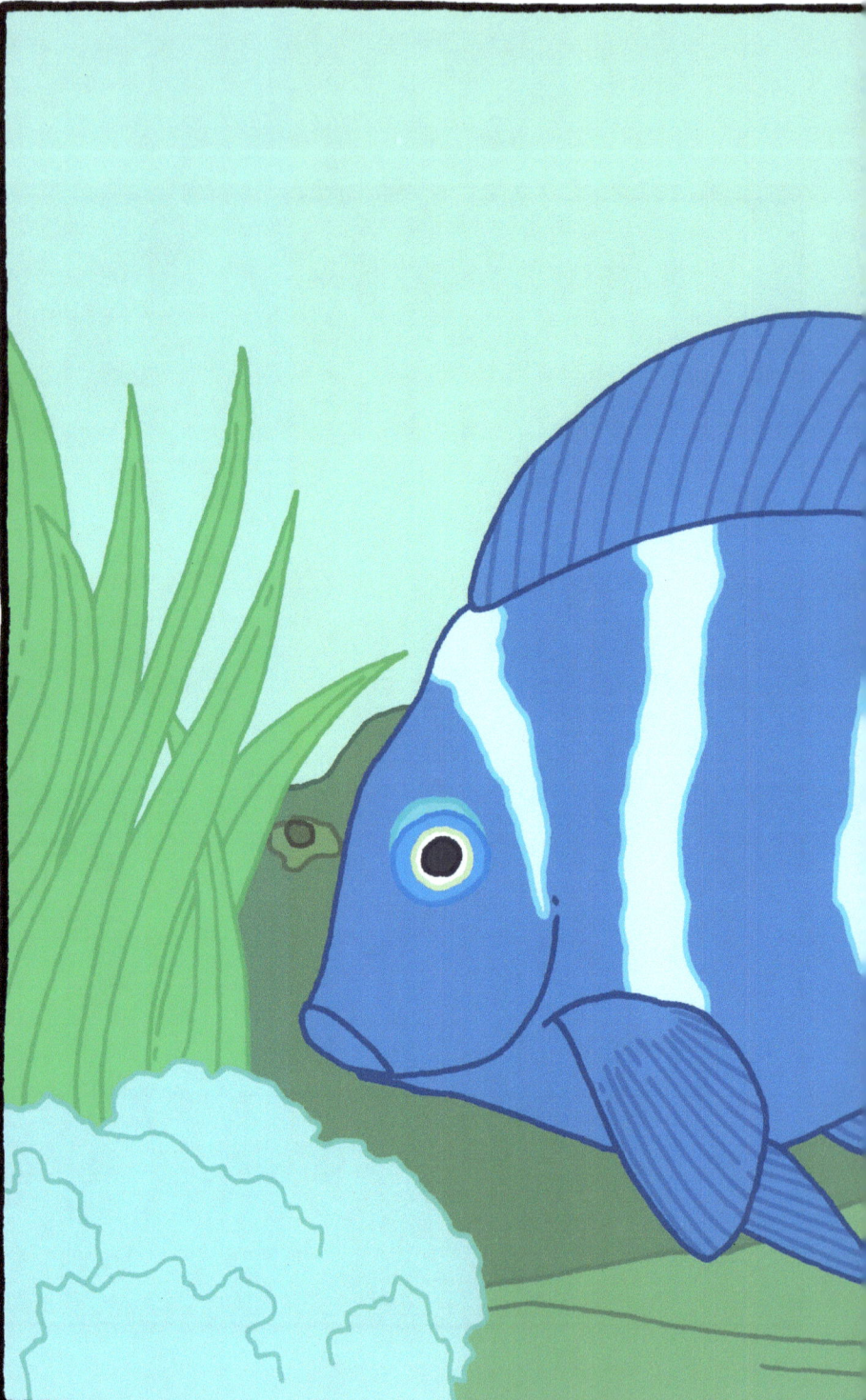

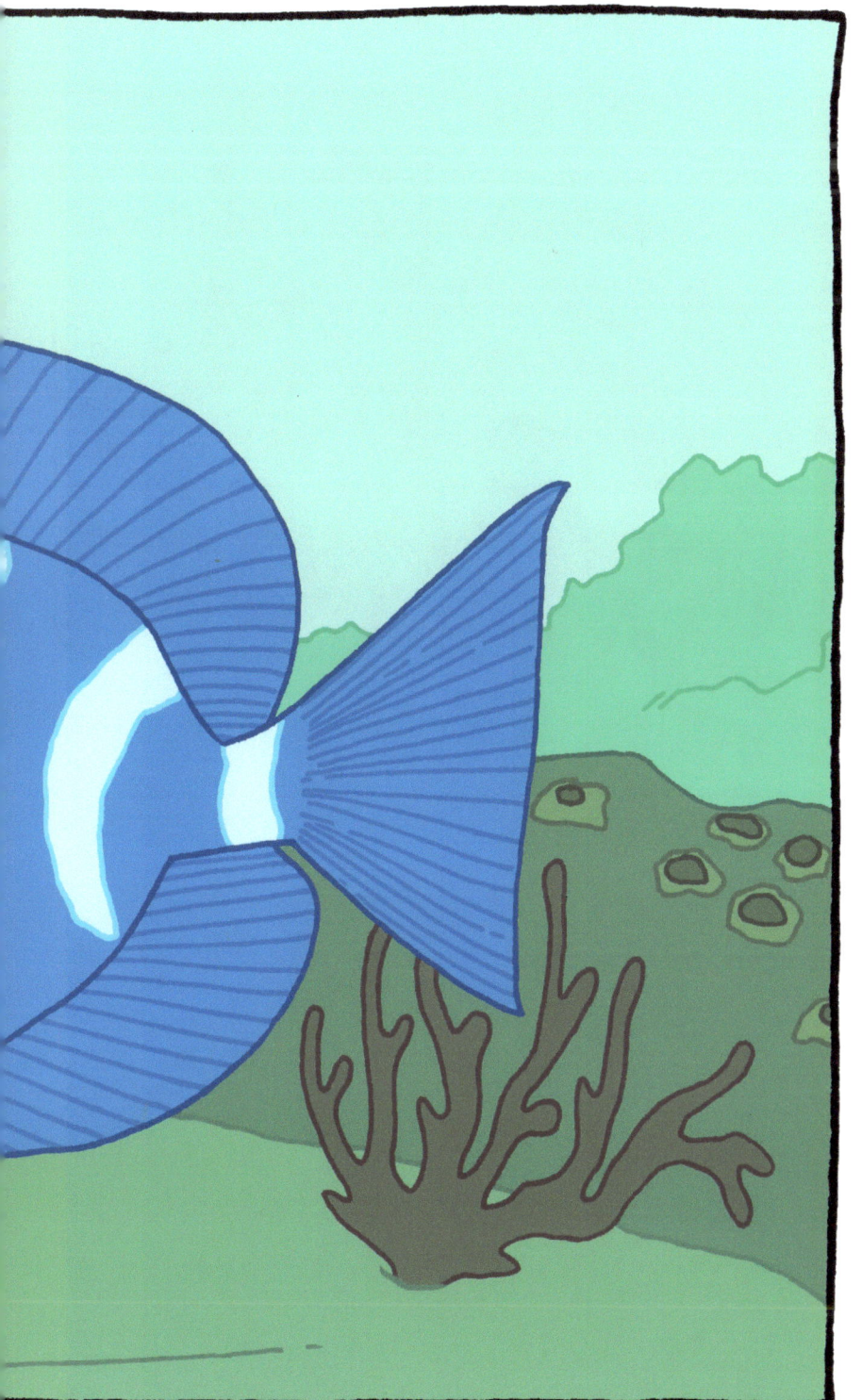

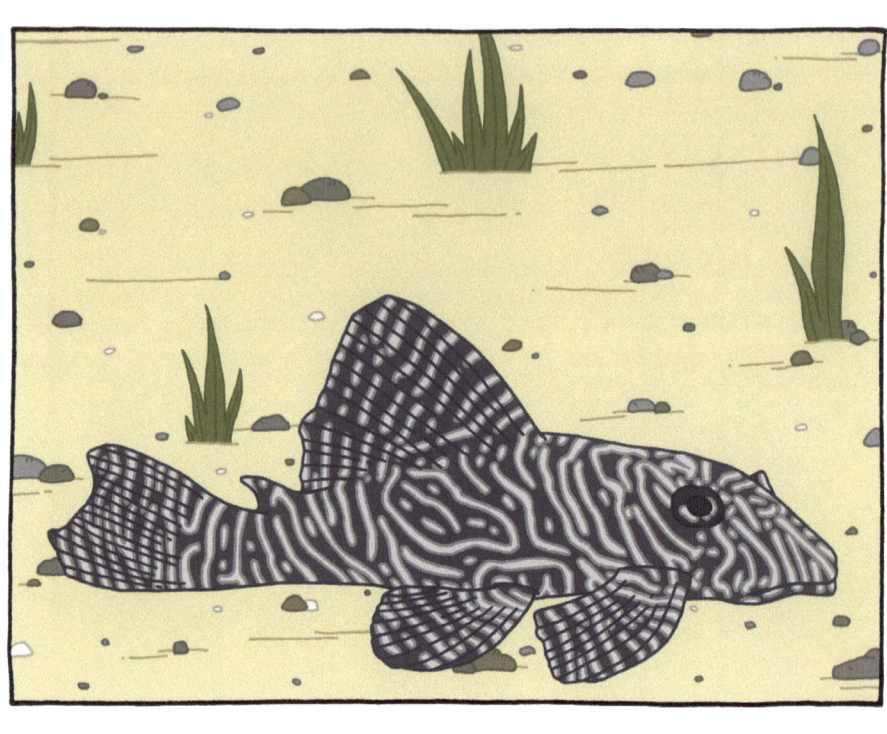

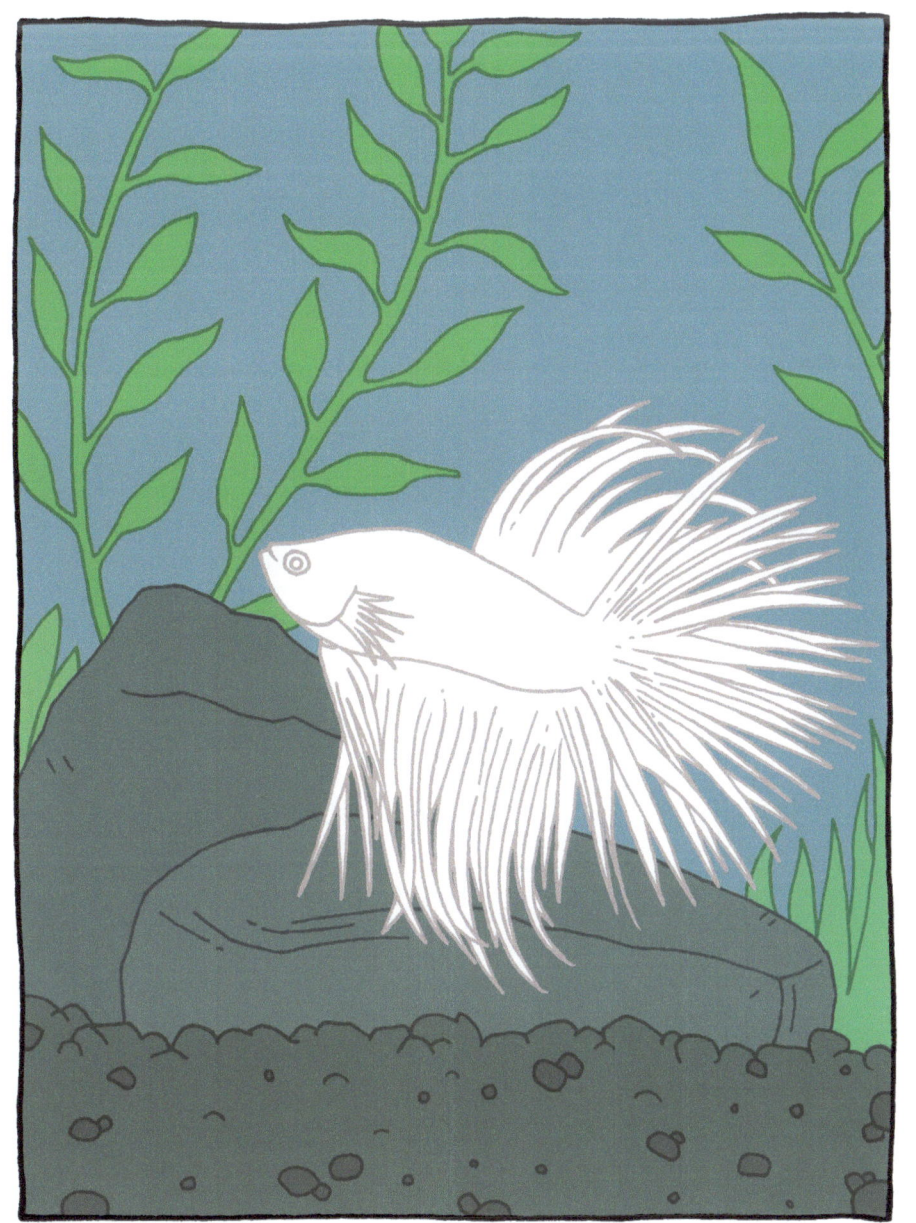

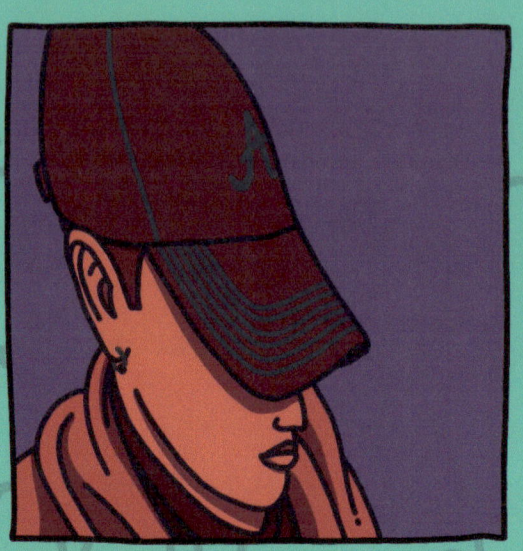

Nathan Lumm has spent the last 20+ years working in both the comic book and advertising industries, but has recently gone out on his own, into the world of freelance illustration. He currently resides in Texas, with his lovely wife and their adorable bunny.

More of his work can be found at:
instagram.com/nathan_lumm
youtube.com/user/lummage

www.ingramcontent.com/pod-product-compliance
Lightning Source LLC
Chambersburg PA
CBHW041209180526
45172CB00006B/1220